Finding Time for Fatherhood

Finding Time For Fatherhood

Due

✓ Out To _____

Finding Time For Fatherhood

Men's Concerns as Parents

❖

Bruce Linton, Ph.D.
Founder of the Fathers' Forum

Berkeley Hills Books
Berkeley California

published by:
Berkeley Hills Books, Box 9877, Berkeley CA 94709
www.berkeleyhills.com

distributed to the trade by:
Publishers Group West

cover design by:
Elysium Design, San Francisco

Library of Congress Card Number: 00-108947

Library of Congress Cataloging-in-Publication Data

Linton, Bruce.
  Finding time for fatherhood : men's concerns as parents / Bruce
Linton.
      p. cm.
  ISBN 1-893163-18-0
  1. Fatherhood. 2. Fathers. 3. Father and child. 4. Parenting. I.
Title.
  HQ756 .L544 2000
  306.874'2—dc21
                                                    00-011337

CONTENTS

PREFACE — WHY THIS BOOK?

Reading these essays and sharing them with your partner as well as with other dads can help you deepen your personal experience of fatherhood. A special feature is the inclusion of questions at the end of each chapter to guide your self-reflection and stimulate discussion.

This book can be used in a number of ways:

- Expectant dads and newly "born" fathers — as well as dads with young children — will find this book helpful in developing a personal understanding of the challenges and tensions we encounter as fathers and parents.

- Couples will benefit as well, allowing mothers especially to catch a glimpse of the transitions and struggles that fathers experience.

- Fathers' groups and men's groups will be able to use these essays to stimulate discussions and explore their experiences as fathers and men.

- Childbirth and parent educators will find the themes reflected in these essays useful as resource material and as a way of getting students to think about the tensions fathers face in becoming parents.

- Obstetricians, pediatricians, and family practice physicians will find this book helpful in introducing the dads they encounter to the normal anxieties men experience when they become fathers.

This is not a "how-to" book. It will not tell you how to burp a baby or change a diaper. Rather, it is intended to stimulate your thinking about what exactly it means to be a father, and what value you place in your own life on being a parent.

This book is dedicated to my father Hyman E. Linton. In his own way, as he answered my questions about his life as a father, my life came into sharper focus. His vision of the future, and belief that "whatever comes his way" he could find a way to work things out, have been my guiding philosophy in life.

Special thanks to John Harris who helped in very large measure to get this work published. I am grateful for our friendship.

Thanks also to the following friends, family, and colleagues for their continual support of my work and the Fathers' Forum: Gayle Peterson, Ph.D., Paul Minsky, Ph.D., Fortunee Stuart, Ph.D.; my very special sisters Phyllis Greene, LCSW and Natalie York, who have always been incredibly loving and caring for me and my family; Scott Linton, MD and Marc O'Krent, who both attended one of my early workshops and put to practice, in their own families, what it means to be a loving and nurturing father; David Akullian, MFT, Paul Moore, Ph.D., Paul Zipperman, MFT, Elayne Savage, Ph.D., Barbara Lewis, MFT, Robin Fine, Ph.D., Steven Ades, Mark Feldman, Bob Shelby, MFT, and Michael Moors, who have all given me words of encouragement in my work; Nadine Antin and Coleman Colla for their warmth and parenting help with my own family; Alan Canter and Irv York for putting up with my golf game!—and for sharing their own struggles and insights into fatherhood; Andrew Samules and Sam Osherson, Ph.D. for their important work with fathers and kind words of encouragement.

I wished it might have been different for Rita and me; I know the love we had and have for our children is real; for her, and our children, Morgan and Julia, this book is a glimpse into the life of our family.

Bruce Linton, Ph.D.
Berkeley, California
October 1, 2000

INTRODUCTION

This book is written as an experiment to reach out to fathers in a unique way. Through my daily work with fathers I have become aware of certain questions and observations about what it means to be a father. Being the parent of two children myself, I have observed how much I have learned about myself through being their father. I have conducted research and read much of the current literature on fatherhood.

The "why" of this book lies in the attempt to combine the research, literature, and my own clinical work with fathers into a book about the important concerns we have as fathers. I have tried not to give suggestions on how to be a father but I have at the conclusion of each essay asked you to consider three questions about fatherhood. This book is written to begin a dialogue both with other dads, and more importantly with yourself, about what being one means to you.

The "why" of this book also derives from the fact that there are many more books about parenting and motherhood than about fatherhood. But, of course, mothers can benefit from this book too. It will give women a chance to hear the man's side of the experience.

The evolution of the modern American family, where both parents are employed, has created the necessity and the opportunity for American fathers to participate more directly in the early years of their children's lives. Today's dad is expected to be a more equal partner, a co-parent, in raising his child. But there is more "in it" for men today than just the "chores" of babysitting. When men discover that parenting gives them purpose and meaning in a way no other experiences can, then "babysitting" and "childcare" are transformed into the substance of fatherhood. Becoming a more caring and compassionate person, knowing your life does make a difference and that you can make an impact on the world — this is what fatherhood is all about. Even with all the stress and frustrations that come with the early years of parenting, and all the lifelong adjustments that we need to make, it is still obvious that nothing humanizes us as men more than being able to care for our children.

In the fathers' group that I lead, many fathers comment on how they never had any close contact with their own fathers, a fact that makes them aware of how important being present in their children's lives is. Other fathers say that being with their children feels like a more creative option than potential career advancement.

As new fathers begin to take on more of the day-to-day care of their children, they are entering what has traditionally been "women's territory." Many fathers that I have worked with say that after trying to develop a close relationship with their newborns, they find themselves retreating to a more traditional role, and fear that they will become the distant fathers that they themselves had. It has become quite clear to me that if men are to develop closer relationships with their children and to be more involved in the workings of their families' daily lives, then they have a lot to learn. And men are going to have to help each other out and educate themselves about the deep satisfaction that comes from parenting.

It sometimes seems as if a natural bond between women occurs when they become mothers. Women seem to develop a special deepening of friendship that comes with sharing the experience of motherhood. In contrast, men seem to become isolated from other men as family responsibilities and adjustments are made. Why don't men seek out other fathers for advice and support? Society seems to force men to compete with other men, and they have become intimidated to the point where they are no longer willing to take the risk to make new friendships. As men try to understand their role as fathers, it can seem too overwhelming to reach out to other men. Not having any role models to show them what kind of friendships are available to new fathers leads them to feel that they have to go it alone. Having children, becoming fathers, is such an important event in men's lives, I wonder how they can NOT want to share this event with their male friends!

My clinical research has taught me that when men become fathers, it is crucial to their adult development to be with other fathers to talk about this important life transition and how it is affecting them. Throughout history, men have had opportunities to share their life experiences with other men. Sharing these events has been an important part of men's overall life experiences. Their emotional and psychological well-being has often been anchored in their social relationships with other men. In the last seventy years, the industrial and office-oriented work style in

My clinical research has taught me that when men become fathers, it is crucial to their development to be with other fathers to talk about this transition.

America has caused men to become isolated from each other. This becomes particularly problematic when men become fathers. How are fathers to understand all the many emotional and psychological changes they encounter if they have no one to talk with, share with, and learn from about all the many changes that parenthood entails?

As men begin to talk about their experiences as fathers together, they can begin to build the bridge to the important relationships that men once shared with other men. They can have a common ground of experience on which to relate. A new model of fatherhood can begin to evolve. The importance of exploring and sharing with other fathers is of great benefit not only to men, but also to their children, their mates, their families, and ultimately to American culture and society too.

| 1 |

Becoming a Father and Learning About Friendship

I cannot remember, in my childhood or adolescence, ever thinking about being a father. I didn't think about it, in fact, until my late twenties, when my partner of three years, Rita, asked if we should have a baby. She says that was the only time she ever brought up a subject I did not want to talk about. No other subject we have ever discussed (moving, changing jobs, buying a house) made me feel so ambivalent.

I was twenty-nine years old, Rita was twenty-five, and it seemed an appropriate time to begin a family. We had both grown up in families of four children. I had recently become licensed as a marriage and family therapist in California. Rita was a registered nurse at our local hospital, and at that time she was working in the nursery. What more could I ask for: a wife who was a nursery nurse!

Although I didn't know it at the time, this was the beginning of my journey to the understanding that by becoming a father I would learn about being a man. I was so confused inside. I found myself faced with what I knew to be one of the most important decisions in my life, and in terrible conflict. How I was taught to be as a man, and what I was feeling inside, seemed completely opposed. The uncertain and ambivalent feelings that I was taught to suppress and resist in order to be a man were just too strong to be denied. Looking back to those years, I can now understand that, even before our child had been conceived, something was changing within me.

> *Characteristically, I began to explore my decision to become a father by making lists.*

Characteristically, I began to explore my decision to become a father by making lists. How would our lives be changed by a child? My lists of positives and negatives grew daily. Finally I became aware that this decision would have to be made with insufficient information. I would have to take a leap of faith. I would need to trust something, as yet unknown, inside myself.

I would need to trust that I could live with fear of the unknown. Fear of not really knowing how our child would change my wife, our marriage, or me. Fear of the emotional and financial responsibilities. Fear that we would not have a healthy baby. Fear of a life that was out of my control. I can now reflect back to this time and appreciate how I was coming to know myself as a man — how control and certainty, traits I had long identified with the "masculine," were merely a facade, a defense against the feelings I was having. I now know that those sleepless nights of anxiety about fatherhood were the beginning of learning how to understand my own fear and self-doubts.

Rita and I took the decision to have a baby very seriously. We went away on weekends and questioned and fantasized about what life with a child would be like. What would it be like to be a family? We eventually both came to an important realization. We had hoped to do some travelling as part of our relationship, perhaps extended trips to Europe, China, or Nepal. Through our discussions, we came to realize that by having a baby we would not be able to indulge ourselves in travelling the way we had planned. We came to understand that by having a baby we would be doing another type of travelling, an inner journey. We would make discoveries about who we were as human beings. At this point, having a child began to feel like an adventure. The hope of pregnancy was transformed into a gift: the miracle of being able to have a baby.

On April 13, 1981, our son Morgan was born. As I held him in my arms in the days that followed his birth, I would often cry. How vulnerable and fragile he seemed. How this little baby would need me! I felt overwhelmed. Was I ready to care for and love this baby? Was I prepared for this most precious of trusts, to nurture a child? How strongly attached to him I felt. How lost I felt about what I was to do as a father.

I was up with him one night when he was about a week old — it was probably about 2 am — and I had turned the radio on. As the announcer read the news, I recall being profoundly concerned about the state of affairs in the world. The world needed to be a safe, welcoming place for my son. War, poverty, crime — these problems needed to be solved . . . immediately!

My son, one week old, was already bringing me into contact with the world in a new way. New feelings of concern and compassion were being born within me. Since he was born, my interest in the environment, schools, the economy and public safety has grown intensely alive within me. It was as if my personal sense of isolation were coming to an end and a new feeling for community beginning to develop.

I was proud and excited to become a dad, but I also felt overwhelmed and bewildered about my life. My wife and I talked about our experiences together, but something was missing for me. I began to realize that she had many women friends with whom she could talk about what it was like to be a mother. I discovered that I had no men friends with whom I could talk and share my feelings about being a father.

I realized that what I needed was to talk with other fathers. I needed to hear from other dads how they were coping with all the changes in their lives and relationships.

This has been one of the most important insight for me as a father: I need to be with other fathers. This insight led me to help form a group for new fathers. The impact of this small group of men took me out of my isolation and also helped me have a forum for the feelings I was either trying or longing to express to my wife. Here in this group of men I had a home for all my confusion and bewilderment about myself as a new parent. Here was a place for me to come and understand myself as a father — and as a man.

FOR FURTHER SELF-REFLECTION AND DISCUSSION

1. Who are your two closest male friends?

2. What efforts do you make to keep in contact with your friends?

3. As a father and a parent, what is important for you to share with another friend/father?

2

From Man to Dad: How Fatherhood Changes Men

The most profound and complicated event in a man's life is becoming a father. It is also the least understood and, until recently, the least researched topic in the study of adult development. No life transition — not getting married, changing jobs, moving, or completing educational goals — will have as long-lasting an effect on a man's sense of purpose as becoming a parent.

When I first became a father nineteen years ago, I thought I was prepared for fatherhood. I had completed my training as a family therapist and was well educated in the stages of the family lifecycle. But I was not prepared for the deep and powerful reorganization of my identity that I would experience. While the changes in my outer world — our daily routines, work schedules, the disorganization in our house, the big changes in the time my wife and I spent together — were very apparent, the feelings going on within me remained mysterious and confusing. It was during our pregnancy, birth, and intense first year of parenting that I began to try to understand the developmental process of becoming a father. It became apparent to me how little information or preparation is available. In retrospect, I realize how helpful it would have been to have a better understanding of this important transition in my life.

Most of us have grown up in families where sharing our feelings was often discouraged.

In our lives today, the major risk factors of pregnancy and birth are not medical. The real risk factor is that the necessary time for the emotional development for both parents and the baby — individually and as a family — will be short-changed. The father, mother, and baby will not get the opportunity to experience the first year together to adjust and learn about their new relationships and roles. Father will be off to work in a week or two, mother will need to return to work after a few months, and the baby will end up in "really good daycare."

Here in the United States we tend to focus on the physical experiences both during pregnancy and birth and in the postpartum period. Discussions about lack of sleep, the baby's feeding schedule, food preparation, and when and whose relatives will be visiting become the focus of many new parents' early experiences. We are often out of touch or ignore our own inner experiences. Most of us have grown up in families where sharing our feelings was often discouraged. In times of stress or change, we have been taught in our families not to talk about our feelings and hold them inside and be stoic. This is particularly true for us as men.

In the weeks following the birth of our son Morgan, I found myself feeling bewildered and overwhelmed. As I talked with my wife about my feelings I felt something was missing for me. She was very supportive and caring about what I had to say about being a dad, but still I felt I needed more. I chose to organize a workshop for expectant and new fathers called the "Fathers' Forum." In fliers that I sent out and posted around my town (Berkeley CA) I described the workshop as follows: "The Fathers' Forum will present a workshop for expectant and new fathers, as well as men who are considering becoming a parent. This is an opportunity for us as men to meet together and explore what it means to become a father. We live in a society/culture that promotes competition and isolation among men. Rarely do men find time to discuss their inner reflections, ambivalence and doubts with each other. This workshop is an opportunity to have a dialogue with a community of men about fatherhood."

Since 1986, I have conducted nineteen of these workshops, with anywhere between six and twenty-two men attending. One of their most revealing features has been that the men consistently expressed anxiety and concern that something was wrong with them, or that they must be abnormal because they were feeling so confused about becoming or being new fathers. The men who attend really were desperate to hear how other new and expectant dads were doing. Most of the men shared in their concluding remarks that hearing the other fathers' stories about the difficulties and struggles they were having helped them realize that they were experiencing "what every new dad goes through."

> *The dads who have attended my workshops often comment on how isolated they feel from other men/fathers.*

The dads who have attended my workshops (or the ongoing

fathers' groups I also offer now) often comment on how isolated they feel from other men/fathers. Most of the men said they turn to their wives, not other men, to help them understand their feelings about fatherhood. With time I have come to understand that men/fathers share feelings quite easily when it is safe to do so (popular preconceptions notwithstanding), but what we as a community of men find especially lacking is the opportunity to have such meetings where the primary focus is on our feelings about being fathers.

Through the workshops and research I have conducted I have identified "Four Phases of Paternal Development."

Through the workshops and research I have conducted I have identified "Four Phases of Paternal Development." Each of these phases offers the man/father a unique opportunity to understand himself through his feelings rather than through his thinking about who he is. Often, when these two ways of "knowing" diverge, tension about our identity results. I see this as a healthy tension, one that is moving us towards a more integrated understanding of who we are as both a thinking and feeling human being.

(1) The first emotional transition involves the man's understanding and resolving his relationship with his own father. (2) The next concerns the way confusion and emotional uncertainty, usually at pregnancy or birth (or through adoption or becoming a stepparent) present him with an opportunity to become more flexible or more rigid as a man. (3) Third is the ability to be dependent and allow others to be dependent on him. (4) The last is how is he able to form affiliations with other fathers and move from isolation to community.

All these transitions lead the man/father to a greater sense of purpose in his life — what I like to call a deepening of his soul. Fatherhood can humanize a man like no other experience I know. The most profound contribution we have to give as men can be our parenting of the next generation. Ultimately, when we reflect on who we are as men, we must ask how have we affected the lives of others.

(1) Masculinity and fatherhood are socially constructed. As times change, our expectations and constructs for who we are as men adapt to the social and cultural needs of our families. This social flexibility is a positive quality for us as men. It liberates us from having to model ourselves after the past, and gives us the freedom to create what is most relevant for us and for our families today.

This is not easy work. Many dads fear that, because their own father was not a "role model" for them, they don't know how to parent. The relationship a man has with his own father is one of the underlying themes he needs to resolve to become, not only the father he wants to be, but also the man he wants to be. Our own independent psychological life is not easy to achieve. The influence of our mothers and fathers runs deep. As men become fathers, their relationship with their own fathers seems to intensify. The working-through of the issues between father and son continues even after the father's death.

Recently, I was consulting with a father in my psychotherapy practice whose father had committed suicide. He came into therapy because his wife had been concerned about his seeming lack of interest in their young son. At first he complained about how much work demanded of him and how he was just tired, not uninterested in his son. He also remarked that when his son became more complex and "interesting" — maybe around five — he was sure he would have a closer relationship with him. All of these insights seemed superficially reasonable. When I asked him about his own father, he had a very strong reaction.

His father had been quite involved with him as a baby and a young child. He had very positive memories of his father and of the pride his father felt for him. His attachment to him was quite strong. He said that his father's suicide took him by complete surprise and he was depressed for a couple of years afterward.

The more we talked about his father, the more the loss of this close, important relationship seemed to dominate his life. He had found it difficult after his father's death to develop close relationships. Not until he met his wife and experienced her steadfast commitment to him could he trust that people could be depended on. He began to recognize that the loss he felt from his father's unexpected suicide had completely undermined his confidence and trust in people. If he couldn't count on his father, whom could he trust? And as the therapy progressed he recognized with sadness and tears that he was keeping a distance from his own son to protect him. He was trying to protect him from what had hurt him the most — the loss of his father. He realized that if his son was not close or attached to him, he would need not suffer the pain of losing someone so dear, so important.

Childbirth and parenting . . . have often been referred to as the "crisis" stage in the couple's relationship.

When he could understand that he was projecting his pain

and loss onto his relationship with his son, another wave of sadness overcame him. He realized how much his son needed him. He became aware of how he was holding himself back from giving his son what he needed — his alive, alert, and interested father. He said it was as if he was treating his son as though he himself were already dead! The therapy continued, and as he experienced the depth and grief of his feelings for his own father, he became able to enjoy and parent his own son. He began to separate out his feelings of himself as a father from his feelings about his relationship with his own.

Although this may be a dramatic example, the pattern is clear with every man I have spoken with over the years. When they became fathers, the need to understand the relationship with their own dad was a psychological step necessary to achieving their own autonomy.

(2) The second transition that occurs through parenthood and adds dimension to men's character is when they confront the change and disorganization that a child brings into their life. As I mentioned earlier, to be masculine is to be in control. We have been socialized as boys to feel that control of our emotions is what makes us strong and desirable. In order to maintain that sense of control we need to cut ourselves off from about half of our emotional life — the fears and worries we all encounter.

Childbirth and parenting brings with it such uncertainty. It has often been referred to as the "crisis" stage in the couple's relationship. I think this term "crisis" misrepresents what is really happening. The connotation of "crisis" is that something has occurred that shouldn't have, and now we need to make things normal again by returning to the situation before the crisis.

In my research I called this transition to parenthood phase for men the "emergent" phase. It seems that rather than a "crisis" occurring, a new definition of the man as a father is "emerging." He cannot go back to the way he was before, and must attain new potential in himself as a father. This new potential asks him to give up a degree of self-centeredness.

Before they have children, both men and women often don't realize how much flexibility and free time they have. After the baby is born, this is so severely reduced that it is probably the most difficult transition the couple has to make — understanding that their life now involves a third person, who, particularly in the early years, needs one-on-one care. Responding to this transition can humanize us.

Being independent, focusing on their own needs, not being "committed," is often depicted in the media as a romantic and attractive lifestyle. Hollywood worships the "eternal adolescent." The man who becomes a parent is usually dealt with in a comic fashion. We don't have a positive and life-affirming image of men as young or new fathers. We don't see fatherhood being pursued as a life choice for men. Finding value, fulfillment and creativity in parenthood is not an image Hollywood has found a way to cash in on.

The confusion and uncertainty brought about by birth and the early years of parenting challenge a man to love and value others outside of himself. It challenges a man to feel himself as part of a group, his family, whose survival and emotional well-being he is part of.

I remember a young father I was seeing as he and his wife were preparing to become parents. He was certain that having a baby would not slow his life down. He was planning on taking up windsailing soon after the baby was born. He had also planned a trip to Mexico for them when the baby would be about six weeks old. He was unable to see that having a baby would change his routines, and that by making plans he was reassuring himself that he needn't look at the confusion and uncertainty he was feeling.

After returning from a very difficult trip to Mexico, getting little sleep, unable to do the things he used to while on vacation with his wife, he was wondering what had happened to their life. In the weeks that followed he was able to admit that not only wasn't he prepared for parenthood, he had no idea what to expect.

Out of the confusion and uncertainty that this young father fought hard against, he regained a sense of working in the present, and grew more focused on his current experience, and what it meant to him now. Maybe it was a matter of survival, but his personality was shifting. At the end of

> *The third transition a man undertakes when he becomes a father is allowing himself to be dependent on others.*

therapy he was a less driven person; he seemed more at peace with the disorganization at hand. He commented on how much closer he felt to his wife and child. He still had plans and adventures for the future, but they did not take him away from the present. In our final sessions he talked a lot about how becoming a father had centered him in his life and day-to-day experience. He was much less concerned with proving to others what an exciting and interesting person he was. Instead, he seemed more open to change, and more aware of the value of his everyday experiences with his wife and child.

(3) The third transition a man undertakes when he becomes

a father is allowing himself to be dependent on others. As John Wayne personified the man who could do it all for himself, today's dads need to be able to value the need for others to depend on and be depended on.

It is becoming clear to couples today that economic survival is interdependent. Both husbands and wives need to work. There is more gender equality in the workplace and home. Men have begun to appreciate that today it takes two parents working together, depending on each other — often just to get by financially. But more than financial dependency, it is emotional dependency that is changing men.

As men we have been raised to believe that if we need to depend on someone we are weak, helpless, and, worst of all, powerless. The old joke about "no matter how lost a man may get he'll never ask his wife for directions" illustrates the idea!

When men feel the vulnerability of their own children it can lead them to an appreciation for how much each member of a family needs each other and how much they depend on others to feel whole. The opposite can also happen. Fear of the vulnerability and defenselessness a man encounters in his own child can cause him to shut down, become removed. It is a powerful experience to realize we were all once at the mercy and good wishes of adults to guide us and nurture us till we could care for ourselves. If we as men were never able to feel we could depend on others, then having others depend on us seems almost intolerable.

In a special case I consulted on, this dependency became alarmingly clear. This man had a three-year-old son and came into therapy with his wife because they were having difficulty with their sex life. They were not having sex very often and he was both angry (which he expressed quite well) and hurt (which he hid equally well). He demanded that his wife agree to have sex at least twice a week or he would either leave her or start having affairs. This was a tense and frustrated couple both sexually and emotionally. She also felt like she wanted to have sex more but often felt exhausted, and more like the housemaid than his wife. As we talked, it became apparent that in a marriage that is monogamous he was dependent upon his wife for sex. No matter what threats he made, no matter what other plans he might act on, if he wanted to remain monogamous (and in this case, married) he had to see that he needed and depended on his wife sexually. He struggled with the idea that he would have to depend on another to get his needs met.

We explored this theme of dependency. It took us back to his childhood, when he was the good little boy who didn't need anyone. He remembers how his parents use to comment on how he was so mature that he hardly needed them. He began to understand how difficult it was for him to "ask" and not "demand" when he required something. In fact, the couple had never had a dialogue about their sex needs in the relationship. It had been an argument about who was not being responsive to whom.

Over time he worked, as did his wife, through the dependency needs they had with each other. He began to feel more permissive with his son. He felt more comfortable with his son's fears and immature behavior. At one point in the therapy he commented on how he was going to give him time to grow up and not be rushed — as he had been.

(4) The fourth transition from man to father is the most difficult, but perhaps the most rewarding. It is also a transition that can make the other three transitions much easier. Understanding our relationship with our fathers; moving through the uncertainty that parenthood presents; understanding our de-

pendency needs — all are phases leading us to be more emotionally caring, kind, and empathetic men. When we can share this journey of adult development with other dads we can learn from each other's experiences. I believe it is the isolation that we as men grow up with, the real lack of contact with other men, that makes our emotional lives so difficult to develop. We have to figure out so much on our own. It is hard to imagine that when we become fathers — the most important transition in our lives — we are often without other men to share and learn with.

This fourth phase is the affiliation phase, where we must find a way to connect with greater community. Part of this happens naturally when our kids enter kindergarten or first grade. We naturally meet other men. But in the early years of parenting, when it is most essential to have the support of other fathers, we are often alone.

The fourth phase is the affiliation phase, where we must find a way to connect with greater community.

In the fathers' groups and workshops I conduct, the old adage that men don't express their feelings just doesn't hold true. The fathers in my groups are overflowing with emotion on all the "transitions" I have just written about. What is missing for these men is not that they have difficulty expressing their feelings, but that they have few or no opportunities to do it. In a safe environment free from competition and one-upmanship, focusing on the importance of parenting, rich and important stories are told. Fears about the instability of marriage, angry, sad and abusive stories of our own fathers, stillbirths and abortions, work and family issues, dealing with in-laws, finding time for ourselves and our wives, concerns for schools and the environment, the meaning of sex in our lives — all are topics which father-to-father we discuss, argue, cry, and laugh about together.

The men who come to these groups have to go to some trouble to be involved. It is not easy, readjusting schedules and having the willingness to make a commitment to a group of men. Concerns about how to have a close relationship with other men are often difficult to understand. What comes out of this experience with other fathers? The men have remarked that talking about fatherhood with other dads has certainly given them more confidence in parenting. They also are clear that they understand much more about who they are as men. When I ask them how fatherhood has changed them as men, the response has been they feel they are more sensitive, compassionate, tender, warm and understanding.

Our children, our wives, our society will all benefit from the wonderful group of truly good men that our children (and ourselves, dad-to-dad) have helped us become.

FOR FURTHER SELF-REFLECTION AND DISCUSSION

1. How has fatherhood changed you as a man?

2. What has been most rewarding about being a dad, and what have you worried about most?

3. What phase of fatherhood are you in now?

Aspects of the Father's Impact on Individual Psychological Development

Through infancy, childhood, and adolescence, we are dependent on our parents to help us gradually learn how to cope with the world around us. They are there to admire us, stimulate us, protect us, and teach us in ways that are attuned to our tendencies and help our creative talents emerge. I believe it is the primary task of parenting to teach children the skills for living that allow each child to deal with the difficulties and disappointments in life without being overwhelmed. I am going to discuss how fathers participate in some unique ways in facilitating this learning.

In terms of interpersonal relationships, the father facilitates the young boy's social learning about communicating and relating to others. Boys with fathers who can be emotionally present and warm acquire interpersonal skills that allow them to find satisfaction in developing attachments with others. The father is indispensable in helping his son with the integration of his aggressive feelings and the activation of what Jungians call the heroic process.

When dads are not emotionally present for boys, especially at adolescence, they have no one to form a positive same-sex identification with, and either cannot separate from their mother, or must devalue her. Often in devaluing their mother to define their own sense of maleness, they must alienate all that is feminine within them. The father is instructive in helping boys find satisfaction in their creative efforts, and assists them in developing a sense of intimacy through both achievement and participation with others. Without this guidance and instruction, often the only intimate feelings men develop is through their sexuality. The hormonal changes at adolescence provide a new challenge to the developing self. Having a father who can help a boy find satisfaction in his creative achievements can enable the son to see his libidinal energy manifest in ways other than sexual.

Fathers offer their daughters an alternative to the equation "woman = mother."

For girls, the first male relationship in their life is their father. He helps facilitate their self-esteem through active support of their interests. Since it is well accepted in our culture that men and males are the "special," privileged ones, what fathers take interest in is automatically of value. A father choosing to participate in the events in his daughter's life confirms that she is a priority for him and thus something of value.

Fathers offer their daughters an alternative to the equation "woman = mother." A father's emotional support validates and confirms the daughter's ability to negotiate in the world. If a father is aware of the erotic feelings stimulated in him by his daughter and doesn't act them out, he confirms her plurality of being: she can be something other than a mother. He facilitates her exploration of other dimensions of her personhood. Critical is the father's respect for the necessary privacy and modesty in order to allow his daughter's developing self to emerge. A father's role in menses is important to mention. This initiation into womanhood is the mother's ritual but the father must be able to mirror this transition positively in support of his daughter's developing sexuality.

Within the construct of the developing sense of work and career and its place in one's life, the father's support and interest are important. His own attitude toward his achievement seems to be the key factor. A father must continue to develop his own talents and interest to find satisfaction in his own life. This is the only way to communicate this potential to his children.

There are many negative stereotypes fathers have to overcome.

There are many negative stereotypes fathers have to overcome. Fatherhood appears to be a social construct adapting and changing to the social and economic conditions of the times. It becomes the responsibility of men as a community to address the needs, desires and aspirations that fatherhood entails for us. Men and fathers today are sincere and courageous in their consciousness-raising and self-reflection in asking themselves: In what ways do we contribute meaningfully to the societies to which we belong?

Not that long ago, there was a strong cultural belief in God and a political hierarchy of kings. We have lost those structures as social supports — in many cases for the better. We now live in a more equitable democratic world. But with the loss of God and king, these layers of "father projection" have fallen on the ordinary everyday dad. How does the everyday father inspire and guide his children in these morally challenging times?

Margaret Mead once said, "Men are a biological necessity but a social inconvenience." How do we move as men into elevating the status of parenting, when the unconscious sentiment devalues our ability to nurture?

The case vignettes that I am going to present reflect some of the important themes I see in relation to the father's impact on individual development. I will focus on the areas of interpersonal relationship, gender identity, and career choices.

I believe that the psychotherapy experience offers a "do-over." A "do-over" is what in my childhood we used to call a play in baseball, kickball or football, where we couldn't decide on the fair outcome of the play, so we would agree to take the play over. In psychotherapy, the client has the opportunity to return to the feeling-states where the essential process of their self was frustrated or where developmental arrests occurred.

In psychotherapy, the client has the opportunity to return to the feeling-states where the essential process of their self was frustrated or where developmental arrests occurred.

The needs and vulnerabilities that were developmentally impaired, in the essential early experiences, can be re-experienced within therapy with different outcomes. New internal psychological structure can form. And if the psychotherapist is good enough, a new paradigm of development can emerge. (It's never too late to have a happy childhood!)

These cases center on what I would consider to be "father material." The first case I want to consider shows how a man's relationship with his own father can become reenacted with his child. In my work with fathers, I have found that understanding the relationship with their own father is central to their experience of parenting. I will refer to my client as Reed in this case vignette.

Reed and his wife came to therapy at his wife's insistence. His wife Mary talked about how supportive Reed had been during the pregnancy and how close she had felt to him. Now that their baby was here he seemed to be preoccupied with work and uninterested in both her and their new baby.

Reed commented that, now that he was the only one working, he felt under a lot of pressure to provide financially for the family. He felt she did not understand that by his working he felt he was nurturing his family. He felt that she did not appreciate that this was his contribution.

Mary did want to be appreciative of Reed, and she agreed that perhaps her focus on the baby had made him feel excluded at times. And she was very satisfied that she had the opportunity to stay home with their baby. She was still concerned that Reed seemed emotionally disconnected from their baby.

When I began to ask Reed about his own father, he started to get agitated. He said his father left the family when he was about nine. He remembers his mother and father always fighting about money. His father struggled to be successful at work and was often not making enough money to support the family. Reed had two other siblings who were older. When he talked with his bother and sister they also remembered how their early years were always filled with the tension between his parents over money. Reed commented on how his father his entire life had never been successful or satisfied with his work. After his father left he rarely saw him, and when he was 22 his father died, indigent and living in a residence hotel.

Reed said that while both he and Mary were working he felt very secure financially. He said he was very frightened now that the fiscal responsibility was all on his shoulders. He mentioned how he was afraid that, like his father, he would have trouble with work and might also end up losing his family. He cried as he realized that what was true for his father was not really true for him. He had a secure job and a career with a great future. Mary could reassure him that if they had financial problems she too could begin to work again and that she would never abandon him because of money problems, but would help work things out for the two of them.

Reed remarked on how hard he was working to reduce the anxiety he was feeling about how he might experience what his dad did — and how much he did want to be able to feel more connected with Massy and the baby, but was preoccupying himself with work as a buffer to protect them and himself from his fear of financial failure.

As we talked, Reed became aware of how much he was depriving himself of enjoying and feeling close to his wife and baby. As therapy continued Reed began to differentiate his own life and feelings from that of his father's. He became aware of how impactful his father's relationship to money and the family had been on him. He also recognized how different his own life was. He still commented on how, to this day, he continues to feel some of his father's despair, but that he knows it is different for him and that he will also manage to work things out with Mary for his family's sake in ways very different from his dad.

As this example demonstrates, men need to understand their

relationships with their own fathers in order to understand themselves as fathers. In ancient times, fathers would acknowledge their sons' autonomy by giving them their blessing. Today, often in therapy, the father's blessing comes through the son's hard work at deciphering the unique relationship, for better or worse, that he had with his own father. The freedom of emotion that comes when men understand the importance of their relationships with their fathers is critically linked to their enjoyment as parents.

The freedom of emotion that comes when men understand the importance of their relationships with their fathers is critically linked to their enjoyment as parents.

Men as fathers will often either overcompensate for the lack of attention and emotion from their own fathers, or as in this case, try to shield their child from the loss or brutality/abuse they may have experienced with their own fathers by distancing or withdrawing from the relationship.

The second case I would like to present is one of a 55-year-old woman, whom I shall refer to as Jill. Jill was a social worker employed by a large social service agency, where she was having difficulties with her boss. Jill came to the first session and was so exceptionally nervous that she trembled and had a great deal of difficulty speaking. It appeared that although she felt unjustly criticized by her boss, she was not capable of complaining or commenting — in reality, not entitled to. Jill wanted immediate help and was frightened of losing her job.

Jill had a father who was critical of both her and her mother. The family rule was not to question the father. The father was the sole provider for the family, the mother was dependent on him and felt limited in her ability to stand up to him on her own or her daughter's behalf. Although she did well in school and was obviously a very intelligent woman, Jill was discouraged by her father from developing academically. The mother and father gave her the message that finding a man to take care of her was her destiny.

With regard to the circumstances of Jill's father, there are certain factors that are important for our consideration. One is the convention of her time, which assumed that women were dependent on men. Therefore Jill's father may have been threatened by Jill's intelligence and possibilities beyond being a wife and mother. Jill did have a brother with whom the father bonded. The emotional distance between the mother and father may have led to family "taking sides," with the boys on one side and the girls on the other. That Jill did not marry and have a family may have been all she could do to individuate herself from her mother, particularly because her father was not able to help her get beyond the assumption that "woman = mother." Jill was an attractive woman and her father may also been threatened by her developing sexuality during adolescence. This might have led him to create increased distance from her.

Jill had never seen a male therapist, although she had been to therapy on and off for many years. I was very interested in hearing Jill's difficulties, something she had rarely experienced with a man. She often felt that she should be "taking care of me," and would often minimize her distress so as not to upset me. When I was able to interpret this, we could go deeper into her feelings. (And I would often reassure her that I was here for her and that I was fine, and if I had any difficulties I could talk with my consultant or therapist.)

Central to Jill's case was the lack of entitlement. The "do-over" that transpired in the therapy and was most helpful for Jill involved (on my part) supporting Jill in her professional development and (on hers) permitting a man to value her intellectual abilities. Together we worked on a letter which Jill sent to the program director commenting on her difficulties with her boss. She asked to be transferred to another position. She was able to transfer to a job she felt much better suited for without any loss of pay. Jill was well received in her new position by her co-workers and found the job more satisfying. A few months later, her old boss was fired. As we worked on Jill's entitlement issues, we worked through not only her mother's passivity with Jill's father, but her own negative introject of her father, which kept her from experiencing career satisfaction. Jill continued to find success at work and eventually sought and found a new job with another company that advanced her career, as well as her career satisfaction.

What was important about our work was that Jill could finally find the recognition, support and admiration for her intelligence and experience. Her positive transference onto me as a man/father substitute for a developmental loss allowed her to give herself, through psychotherapy, the internal positive nurturing father she missed in her family. The critical voice within diminished. The "do-over" of the therapy provided Jill with the paternal acknowledgement she needed to reduce the normal tensions she experienced in the working world. She found she could make the professional transitions that would provide her with satisfaction.

The third vignette is one in which I started see the couple together and then continued on to work with the husband. I shall refer to him as Rex. The couple had come to me to work out some of their early parenting issues, around areas like who gets up with the baby at night, and what is the equitable division of housework and earning money.

Both Rex and his partner had come to be parents in their early 40s. Although Rex was well educated and quite bright, he was marginal in his career and made barely enough money to contribute his half of the monthly expenses. When Rex began working with me alone, he complained about his wife's lack of sexual responsiveness. Having worked with them as a couple, I knew there were some valid concerns in this area. But Rex had received several complaints from women friends about his inappropriate hugs. He would squeeze them too tight and hold them too long. He had also flirted with the idea of having a homosexual affair with one friend who was willing, but finally hesitated about acting on it. On several occasions, Rex's wife asked him to talk to me about the comments he had made at a party or when they had friends for dinner. These comments were often charged with sexual material that others responded to negatively. Rex was always surprised by the negative response and talked about how he was the only spontaneous one in the group. He was a classic borderline personality with narcissistic tendencies.

In two years of individual therapy, we were able to make progress on both Rex's career underachievement and his need to sexualize much of his interaction with others. Both these issues were closely linked with his father. Rex's father, a writer, was, as Rex described him, often moody and withdrawn (depressed). I have seen with many adult men that their career destiny seems to be closely linked with how they viewed their fathers at adolescence. Often fathers experience their mid-life transition as their children become adolescents. At midlife, the acceptance of things not done, goals not met, can erode the father's sense of purpose. His son will pick up on his depression and often internalize this to interpret work as a burden, an overbearing responsibility — a type of indentured servitude. This is related, not so much to the father's achievement, as to his attitude toward achievement. His attitude toward achievement is manifested in his personality, and it is this attitude his children emulate.

I have seen with many adult men that their career destiny seems closely linked to how they viewed their fathers at adolescence.

To further complicate matters, I have observed that, in adolescence, particularly for boys, it is the father's "work" to help them direct their libidinal drive into areas of personal achievement and satisfaction. Writing, artistic exploration, music, poetry, athletics — whatever the endeavors be, these activities help them find a way of relating intimately in the world and finding gratification through achievement. Without this possibility, all that remains is for the sexuality to become the only environment for self-satisfaction.

Rex's parents had a bond from which he often felt excluded, and he also needed to compete with his two older brothers for his parent's attention. He saw his mother's attentiveness to his father manifested mainly through their sexuality. It appeared that the mother would help stimulate the father out of his depression by their sexual relationship. This relationship around sexuality is what Rex viewed as the "good stuff," and the sole demonstration of his father's vitality.

As we proceeded in the therapy, Rex left many sessions discontent. He eventually organized his career and went on to become more at peace with the work world. He even enjoyed moderate success. He worked very diligently on his feelings about his sexuality and ultimately found satisfaction within his marriage. In one of our later sessions he confided in me that he started to work on paintings, and was keeping it secret. He joked that he may not be having as much sex as he would like, but his painting was becoming expansive — and it felt great.

In the fathers' groups I have led, it is apparent that most men look to their own fathers as examples of how to be parents. But reflecting on their own fathers' behavior often leaves them feeling sad, lonely, frustrated, angry and ambivalent. In our group, together, we struggle to understand and make peace with our fathers. Many of the men in my groups feel very limited by having a father who was either physically or emotionally absent from their lives. We try to understand how we can be more available and more emotionally connected with our families. Some of the men who had abusive fathers become fearful and wonder if they might hurt their own children. If we must rely on our own personal fathers as teachers or mentors on parenting, we may feel limited. To understand himself as a man, each of us must come to an understanding of his own father and his father's influence on his life, both positive and negative.

Becoming a more nurturing parent involves more, however, than just understanding our relationship with our father. We have to look beyond them. Where must we look to gain a broader perspective about what it means to be a father ourself?

The idea of an original model after which similar things are patterned — a kind of prototype — is what the depth-psychologist Carl Jung called an archetype. I thought there would have to be a prototype for what it means to be a father, but I was surprised by what I discovered.

There is an archetype for motherhood. The "Madonna and Child" image appears in some form throughout the world. The biological basis of pregnancy and of giving birth sets up a relationship between mother and child that is, to varying degrees, stable in all parts of the world. This is not the case for fatherhood. Images of fathers and their relationships with their children are not stable, but vary widely from culture to culture. If this is true, what does it tell us about the meaning of fatherhood?

Images of fathers and their relationships with their children are not stable, but vary widely from culture to culture.

To begin with, it seems to indicate that fatherhood is socially constructed. Depending upon the culture, the historical time and the needs of the society, fathers may play a variety of roles. It is both a frightening and liberating thought that fathers have no prototypic model for how to be parents. This means that men can stop looking towards (and perhaps blaming) their own fathers for instruction (or lack thereof) on how to be fathers. They can begin to explore within themselves and in the world at large for the kinds of behavior and family life they would like to provide for their own children. They must turn to each other, father to father, and learn together how to develop positive nurturing relationships with their children.

Understanding what it means to be a father is a very personal journey for each and every one of us. Each father, in his own way, must search out and discover what kind he wants to be for his children. It is a difficult journey and many men shy away from questioning what it means to be a father. For those who are willing to take the journey, it is surely a path filled with heartfelt expectations. Hopefully it is a path shared with fellow fathers where, at this time in history, we can help each other along the way. Perhaps never before have we had such an opportunity to consciously participate in the lives of our children.

It's a great time to be a father. Seize the moment!

FOR FURTHER SELF-REFLECTION AND DISCUSSION

1. What social stereotypes do you think your father labored under?

2. Did you feel supported by your father during your adolescence and period of emerging sexuality?

3. If you were to write a letter to your father about how you feel about him as your dad, what would you say?

4

FATHERS AND MARRIAGE

The most important things in life are not things — they are our relationships! The relationship that has had the most impact on our own lives is the one we had with our parents. By the same token, our relationship with our partners — our marriages — will influence our children in many profound ways.

Providing good schools, living in a decent neighborhood, participating in community and sports activities, having a computer, offering music lessons — these are some of the ways we help to nurture our kids as they grow and develop. Every father wants his child to grow up to be an honest and caring person. But how does that happen?

If we reflect on our own parent's marriage, what was it like? Did they treat each other with dignity and respect? Were they considerate and understanding with each other? How did they handle the inevitable anger and frustration that comes not just with parenting, but with life? Did they seem to enjoy being married? Why did they have children?

Marriage and fatherhood are relationships that forces us to reflect on the family in which we grew up. As children, we absorb so much of what goes on around us. We usually are unaware of what or how or when the events and relationships from our past may influence choices, relationships, and responses in our adult lives. Much of the work of dynamic psychotherapy is to help individuals become aware of the long forgotten, now unconscious responses we have to the relationships and events happening in our lives now.

Thinking about our parent's responses in their marriages can go a long way in helping us understand not only how we may respond to our partners, but also what value and meaning marriage offers us. And lucky for us today, more than ever, we can work with our partners to create the marriage that we want. We can evolve beyond the restricted structures and social constraints that may have limited our parent's ability to find a more satisfying relationship within their marriage.

Letting our child see our concern and interest in our partner tells them much about what human relations are based on.

But most important for us as a father is to understand that by caring for and loving our wives we can be offering a great gift to our children. Letting our child see our concern and interest in our partner tells them much about what human relations are based on. And when difficulties do arise, being able to bear the tension and disappointment allows us to stay in the relationship emotionally even when we may not be feeling positive about our spouse. Think about that — that we can love someone and at the same time feel disappointed by him or her. How we encounter and work in our marriage lays the groundwork for what loving potentially means for our children. The relationship between husband and wife is the center of a child's developing morality. How he treats himself and others grows out of the observations he makes of the way his parents treat each other.

Many men who become fathers today take pride in their involvement, right from birth, in the nurturing and caring of their infants. This is a very positive change in our culture.

The relationship between husband and wife is the center of a child's developing morality.

Fathers' involvement in active parenting is creating a new model for family life.

I am always struck by meeting fathers who are so positively engaged with and excited about their children, but appear so uninterested in or disengaged from their relationships with their wives. I often comment to couples whom I see in my psychotherapy practice that they act like single parents who are living together. Everything in their relationship seems to focus on their child.

In many cases, as time goes on, the parents begin to work out many of their interpersonal difficulties through their children. Young children may begin to wonder why their parents seem to have so much love for them and not seem to care much about each other. What does an experience like that teach a child about interpersonal relationships?

And sometimes marriages need to change. At times, for specific reasons, a couple finds out that they are not able to work out their difference. Most couples with children try to go the extra mile to make their family's work, but it is not always possible. Sometimes the interpersonal issues from our family of origin are just too mismatched with our partner's character, and no matter how hard the two people try, they cannot resolve the tension and frustration they feel with each other. If they can value their roles as parents, then they can make the transitions that are necessary, not only to separate or divorce, but also to keep the parenting support their children need to survive and thrive. Some marriages are just not sustainable. It is no shame or cause for blame if a marriage can't be maintained. We can try and provide our children with the example of two sincere and loving people who are trying to work at life's challenges, while still considering their children's best interests.

There is a great renaissance today for men, and today's father is the cornerstone. A new developing sense of masculinity and gender identity is unfolding around the development of the nurturing father. It is important, rewarding and valuable to participate in the caregiving of our children. But if we don't also nurture our marriage, what have we really conveyed to our children about being a loving and caring person'? One of the greatest gifts a father can give to his children is to love his wife. This is a lovely statement, but in reality a difficult and often lifelong adventure in understanding another person.

FOR FURTHER SELF-REFLECTION AND DISCUSSION

1 . What is most difficult for you about loving another person?

2. What are the trade-offs in being married? (What do you find liberating about beings married, or in a committed relationship, and what is restricting?)

3. What can you do in your relationship that would have a positive effect without your spouse changing her behavior or personality?

5

PREGNANCY AND BIRTH

Becoming a father and a parent is a transformational process for a man. When a man becomes a father, he comes in contact with a deep paternal masculinity through loving his child, partner, and family. When a child enters a man's life, a new depth of feeling and emotion is awakened within him. Growing up male in the United States is for many men an education in how to deny his feelings. From an early age we are taught not to cry, not to feel dependent, but to be in "control" of our emotions.

When we begin to approach fatherhood either by beginning to talk about having a child with our partners, or by hearing those life-changing words, "Honey, I'm pregnant," an emotional avalanche of feelings begins. It is this avalanche of new feelings, which if understood and not feared, can help humanize us as men in the most fundamental and profound way. When we begin the journey toward fatherhood we have the opportunity to recover the nurturing, patient, dependent and tender side of our own personalities that was, for many of us, socialized out of us as we made are way toward adulthood. Becoming a father is our chance to become a man who is truly masculine by being emotionally available for our children and our partners.

In my work with fathers, what I hear new dads talk about most is their interest in being participating and active parents. They want to be able to nurture their child and family by being more than just the bread-winner — as many of their fathers were. They don't want to just put bread on the table for their families, they want to sit down and eat dinner with them too!

When we begin the journey toward fatherhood we have the opportunity to recover the nurturing, patient, dependent and tender side of our own personalities.

A new universe of feelings is awakened in a man through the process of pregnancy and birth. It has been my experience that, although women often appreciate this new awakening of feeling in their spouse or partner, they don't really understand what it means to the new or expectant father.

Men's involvement in pregnancy and birth, and their participation in the early years of their children's lives, have changed dramatically over the past 25 years. In 1965, about 5% of fathers attended the birth of a child. In 1989, almost 95% of fathers were present. Men are clearly asking for more participation in the childbirth process. It is also interesting to note that, according to a recent survey on men and work, 75% of the men would accept slower career advancement if they could have a job that would let them arrange their work schedule to have more time with their families.

At the prospect of becoming a father, men are filled with excitement, fear, wonder, worry, love, and confusion. (To name just a few feelings!) Throughout the pregnancy and birth, the man now becoming a father is trying to find ways to express and integrate these and many more feelings. Since most pre- natal classes focus on the woman's experience in pregnancy, dads often feel that this potpourri of new feelings they are ex- periencing is a sign that something may be wrong with them! Not true. It is normal to feel overwhelmed and insecure about the impending life-changing event of having a child. Worries about finance, time, and how a baby will change your relation- ship with your partner are all normal concerns of "healthy preg- nant fathers."

In recent years, prenatal education has made an effort to understand the fathers' experience during pregnancy and birth. Many programs are now offering classes for dads based on the model that I developed through the Fathers' Forum programs. The key factor for us as men is to be able to talk with other expect- ant and new dads about their experi- ences in this life-trans- forming time. So even if your prenatal classes

The key factor for us as men is to be able to talk with other expectant and new dads about their experiences in this life-transforming time.

don't offer opportunities for you to meet with the dads alone, ask a few of the men in your classes if you can spend some time together and talk about your experiences of the pregnancy and what the birth may be like.

Many men begin during the pregnancy itself to develop bonds with their children. Expectant fathers in my groups have talked about how they enjoyed laying their hands on their partners' bellies and talking to their babies. This very personal and private communication is very powerful as a prenatal bonding ritual. Helping choose the birth attendants, midwife or doctor, and being involved in the choice of where the baby will be born are other ways men begin to get involved.

In my work with fathers, I see men seeking to understand the journey from man to father, and I see how something very special happens when this search for understanding is shared with other men/fathers. Finding a relationship with other men/fathers during pregnancy is an important way in which we can help initiate each other into fatherhood. Seeking out male friends or family members who are willing to share with you their stories of how their life has changed since they have become a father is a way to both prepare yourself for parenthood. It may also help you to begin thinking about the way you will want to be a father.

Men today want to participate in the birth process, and in most cases are expected to share the birth of their child with their partners. They want to be there right from the start to welcome their baby into the world. They want to be involved in offering support and love, and to feel part of the experience with their partners.

I wonder what it will be like for the next generation of children whose fathers attended their births — when our sons and daughters say to us that they are thinking about having a baby, and we can say, "I remember when you were born." And we can tell them what it meant for us to be present at their birth.

Fathers who are able to participate in the birth of their children often report that the sharing of this experience with their partners remains one of the most important moments in their lives. Even — or especially — if the birth is difficult, or a cesarean delivery, men feel strongly about being present at this special time. Sharing the birth experience — its intensity and emotionality — can deepen a couple's bond, as it is one of life's most intimate experiences.

Expectant fathers also need to explore what they need at the birth. What kind of support does the expectant dad need? Many of the new fathers I have worked with talked about how important it was to have a male friend, or other father, with whom they could talk. Beginning to consider what friends and family could be there to understand and appreciate what your feelings are can be very helpful. Thinking about sharing your experiences with someone other than your partner can help. Sometimes new dads are reluctant to share their fears and worries with their partners because they

> *Most dads I have worked with felt much more connected to the pregnancy and birth once they were able to acknowledge the negative feelings that they experienced.*

feel it would be upsetting for her. In wanting to protect their partners from being "hurt" by their worries, dads often neglect these feelings as burdensome or inappropriate. It is best to seek out male friends and other dads to share your fears and negative feelings about becoming a father. We all have them. If it is not comfortable or doesn't feel right to talk with your partner about them, don't let them go unexpressed. Most dads I have worked with felt much more connected to the pregnancy and birth once they were able to acknowledge the negative feelings that they experienced. And most found that other new and expectant fathers were very interested in hearing about them.

"Engrossment" is the term researchers use to describe the father's total absorption and preoccupation with the presence of a newborn. This term could be expanded to describe the early weeks of family life. The first few hours after the delivery are a very important time for the new family to be together. The bonding triangle of mother, father, and baby is configured by all three being together in these first moments of family life.

The most important aspect of family bonding for new fathers is time. If the new father can have the time to be with his partner and child, the natural process of bonding will take place. There is nothing the father needs to do but spend the time with his new family. As fathers get to know their newborns, they often find a new level of feeling is awakened in them.

This too is an especially important time to be with and talk to other fathers about your experience. It can deepen your own experience, as well as validate your growing sense of what being a father is all about. It is important not to be isolated as a new father, and to have other resources than your partner to share the many changes new fathers go through. Being in fathers' group is one way to find affiliation with other men.

A father is looking for a psychologically satisfying place within his family. There are many benefits to his involvement in pregnancy, birth, and the early years of a child's life. These benefits are not only for his child and wife/partner but also for his own understanding of what it is to be man and a father. What I have seen in my work with fathers is that we, as fathers, need to share our experience and support each other. Our dialogue as a community of men helps us understand and appreciate the most important and dynamic life transition: becoming a father.

FOR FURTHER SELF-REFLECTION AND DISCUSSION

1. What training, classes or other preparation did you have for becoming a father?

2. Can you find two other expectant or experienced fathers to meet with, and find out how they feel or felt about the pregnancy of their partners and the birth of their children?

3. After reading this essay, what would be the one question you would like to ask another father about pregnancy or birth?

6

How Having a Baby Changes a Couple's Relationship

When a man and a woman have a baby, it is a profound transition — the most important change in their adult lives. How becoming parents can affect them as individuals and as a couple is still not well understood in our culture. Of all the Western industrialized countries, the United States offers the least support for family adjustment and development. Politicians would like us to believe that we put a priority on family life, but the reality is just not so. How a man makes the transition to parenthood, and how a baby changes a man's relation to his wife, are very important areas for us as men to understand.

When a baby is born, the focus of the new mother's attention is on the baby. This is part of the normal developmental process. Mothers become preoccupied with the baby's needs, often to the exclusion of everyone and everything else. This is part of her biological makeup. Most new fathers are unaware of this normal maternal preoccupation and are often surprised and frustrated at how abandoned they may feel. We have no information about what to expect after a baby is born. Men have very little preparation for this intimate part of life. Childbirth preparation classes often help us share with our wives the experience of pregnancy, but we are unaware of what to expect emotionally after the baby arrives. So what's a dad to do?

As a new father feels the emotional withdrawal of his wife's attention, he can take comfort in knowing that her total attentiveness to their baby is normal. He can begin to notice whether he has feelings of anger and hurt. Often the time after birth may stimulate unconscious feelings that remind the father of his own childhood. But what about his normal needs for attention and intimacy?

Intellectually, a father can become aware that he is participating in an intimate, common and normal experience of the biological foundation of life. He can take comfort in knowing that as their baby adjusts to being outside rather than inside its mother, this intense connection needs to sustain itself for a while.

He can also be active in sharing and bonding with his wife and baby by participating in this great mystery of getting to know himself and his wife in their new roles as parents, and becoming acquainted with this new being called their child. He can begin to get a glimpse of his own vulnerability as the uncertainty of his new role and relationships emerges.

Often the new feelings a man discovers when he becomes a father press him to overwork, perhaps to drink more or to have an affair — all of them ways of trying to escape from the pain of feelings he may be having about the change in relationship with his wife. Even when he is aware of the biological calling for his wife's intense intimacy with the baby, he still feels his own intimate needs neglected.

What I found in my research on new fathers is that throughout history men have had other men — other fathers — with whom to share the transition to parenthood. The joy and loneliness, the fear and confusion were emotions men were able to experience with each other. This was a natural intimacy that men had between them. It is something we have lost in Western industrial countries. Historically, we have always had a community of men friends to turn to at the critical times in our lives. Without this important relationship in a man's life, all his intimacy needs, especially for understanding and comfort, are demanded of his wife and his marriage.

Not only do we need to be able to establish an intimate relationship with a group of men when we become fathers, but throughout our lives we need the companionship and support we can offer each other.

The stereotype of men persists that "they don't share their feelings." What I have found in my work and research is that men don't have opportunities to share their feelings. In my fathers' groups and my all-day workshops we never seem to have enough time to talk, discuss and share all that we want to. The fathers comment on how, unlike their wives — who have many groups available — they have no place to go to specifically talk about the changes they are going through as men and dads.

Not only do we need to be able to establish an intimate relationship with a group of men when we become fathers, but throughout our lives we need the companionship and support we can offer each other. Building and maintaining relationships is not easy with the pace and mobility of life today. For us as men to value our male friends, and to work on developing our relationships with each other, takes commitment. Finding ways to create opportunities to be together to talk about the important experiences we are living is of immeasurable value. Having a community of men friends can profoundly effect the quality of our marriages and how our children feel about us as fathers and men. Maybe the loneliness we feel after our babies are born is not just the change in the relationship with our wives, but the sadness we feel at being without any close men to share this most important time in our life.

FOR FURTHER SELF-REFLECTION AND DISCUSSION

1. How has your relationship with your partner changed since you became parents?

2. Do you feel jealous of your partner's relationship with your child?

3. How do you imagine other couples are affected by becoming parents? Do you think, as men, we have any similar experiences as we become fathers?

7

Sex and Parenthood

Having a baby and making the transition to parenthood is a very complicated process. I say this from both my professional perspective as a family counselor and my own experience as a father of a 16- and a 19-year-old. With all the various pressures on young families, there is often not enough time or energy for parents to have the sexual contact one or both partners desire. As I look back on my marriage (and it's still true today), both my wife and I have had to discuss and accommodate our personal needs and desires, as well as the logistics of work schedules and kids' schedules, to find the time and "timing" to be together sexually.

Before we had kids (which seems like another lifetime now), our sexual relationship was fairly spontaneous. We had time together most evenings, and we were young and had less complicated professional and emotional commitments. Over the years together, just being parents has changed our emotional dispositions, our bodies and our desires for sex. After twenty-three years together, we are truly different people than we were when we met. Our sexual relationship has in its frequency and intensity been rather unpredictable. I have tried to keep an open dialogue about how I feel about our sexual relationship, but at times it has been difficult to discuss. I think each of us has been concerned about hurting the other in discussing our sexual need. My wife and I continue today to struggle with our sexual desires and our needs for intimacy while we try to understand our individual differences, what we need in terms of sex, and how to feel close and connected in our marriage.

How important is sex to a marriage? Sex seems to be the emotional barometer for most marriages. Not in the sense that the more sex the better the marriage, but in the sense that the way couples can discuss openly and with concern for each other their feelings about intimacy is a good index of the health of their relationship.

The way couples can discuss openly and with concern for each other their feelings about intimacy is a good index of the health of their relationship.

In this way, sexuality is a symbolic way each partner becomes emotionally vulnerable. As a psychotherapist, I am acutely aware that each individual's ability to be emotionally vulnerable is often more a reflection of the influences of the family he or she grew up in than of feelings about a current relationship or spouse.

I find in my work that in the couple's relationship, the individuals are working out the intimacy (or lack of it) that they experienced in their own family of origin. Although couples will focus the tension in their relationship on sexuality, that is often a reflection of feelings of being appreciated and understood. What psychotherapists call "being seen" by one's partner — a sense that the other person understands or empathizes with your experience, separate from his or her own — appears to be a significant building block for emotional intimacy. As my clients report to me, there is a high correlation between this type of "being seen" and sexual intimacy and desire.

As my clients report to me, there is a high correlation between "being seen" and sexual intimacy and desire.

In working with fathers I have noticed a few particular themes in regard to sexuality. Some men have difficulty adjusting to the change in their wife's body shape after the birth of a baby. With all the advertising and media hype about how women's bodies should look, the whole Playboy image can create problems for men (and women). Fathers often need to free themselves from the fantasies of the commercialism of women's sexuality to appreciate the reality of their wife's sexuality. During pregnancy, some men begin to resent the attention their wives get. They can develop an underlying anger that can become a powerful inhibitor to feelings of sexuality. After the baby is born, the two-person bond is shifted. A new father often feels excluded by his wife's attention to their newborn. This can lead to feelings of anger, sadness, and depression. Oftentimes these feelings are expressed by either emotional or physical withdrawal. Many men (and women, too) aren't consciously aware of these feelings. It can be difficult to talk about these feelings, even if the parents are aware of them. Especially in the early years, when most fathers are trying to find their place in their families, they may feel it would be a burden on the relationship to discuss the way they feel. They may even feel guilty for having these feelings.

Some men feel uncomfortable about having sex during pregnancy. They have fears they will be hurting the baby or their partners. Many men need to look at how they view their own bodies in relationship to a pregnancy. If, during the pregnancy (this can also be true throughout the marriage), a man's partner agrees to accommodate his physical needs but isn't interested herself in lovemaking, how should he feel? If he is enjoying himself and she isn't, should he feel guilty? Is this kind of sexuality OK?

Is sex necessary? For some couples, it is critical to have an active sex life. It serves as both a physical and emotional outlet for tension. For other couples, the fun and excitement they experience through sex is very important. While many couples need to have sexual intercourse to feel satisfied, other couples find cuddling and holding will suffice. At various times in a relationship, couples feel the need to put their sexuality on hold while they are working through other issues in their life or relationship.

There are many legitimate forms of lovemaking that we overlook. Stress and tension in life are often relieved by feelings of closeness and by holding and touching another human being (most often our partners). Kissing, massage and mutual masturbation are all ways to fulfill physical desires we all normally need to express.

Through working with the sexuality in our marriages we learn about so many things: our needs for closeness and intimacy, our own desires and our own bodies. By discussing these feelings with our partners we gain perspective and develop emotional maturity. We learn that our sexual desires and needs can be a doorway to a deeper understanding of our partners and ourselves.

FOR FURTHER SELF-REFLECTION AND DISCUSSION

1. How has the sexuality in your relationship changed since you had a child?

2. Do you know other dads or men with whom you can talk about your sexual feelings in your marriage?

3. How important to you is the sexual relationship in your marriage?

8

A NEW INTERPRETATION OF AN OLD MYTH: OEDIPUS RECONSIDERED

Sigmund Freud was a physician whose interest in neurology led to the development of modern psychology. He used the Oedipus story from Greek mythology to express how strongly young boys may be attached to their mothers' love. He felt that this story explained what he considered to be an unconscious process in which a young boy rejects his father so that he can have his mother's love all to himself. The Oedipal complex and the Oedipal phase of development have become commonplace in the terminology of childhood psychology. Working through the Oedipal phase, young boys separate from their mothers and begin to develop their sense of themselves as men. Unfortunately, if one accepts the traditional interpretation of Freud, it means that boys must reject their mothers (and the femininity that their mothers represent) in order to develop their own identity and masculinity. This not only devalues mothers and women, but cuts off boys' connections to the feminine principal, which limits their development of a more whole and well-rounded psychological/emotional life.

Let's reconsider the Oedipal myth. The story of Oedipus begins with King Laius and Queen Jocasta of Thebes. Laius learns of a prophecy from the oracle of Delphi that he and his wife will have a son who will kill his father and marry his mother. When their son is born, Laius has the newborn child left on a hillside to die so that the prophecy cannot be fulfilled.

New fathers often report feelings of jealousy because of all the attention the baby is getting and the neglect they feel as a result.

The infant boy, Oedipus, is found by a shepherd and raised by King Polybus of Corinth. Oedipus hears the prophecy as a man and leaves Delphi and Corinth, fearing that he will kill Polybus, who he believes to be his real father. On his journey Oedipus encounters an arrogant, rich nobleman who orders him off the road. Enraged, Oedipus kills the man, who turns out to be Laius. Oedipus ends up outside the city of Thebes, which is terrorized by a Sphinx and can only be saved by someone who can answer the Sphinx's riddle. Oedipus answers the riddle, the Sphinx kills herself, and Oedipus is honored by the whole city. Queen Jocasta has lost her husband and Oedipus is deemed a good match for her, so they marry, fulfilling the prophecy. When Oedipus becomes aware that the prophecy has come true, he blames himself for all that has happened, and blinds himself.

In my interpretation, this myth says more about fathers than it does about boys. It is the father who is jealous and fearful that his son will marry his wife and become king. The father is worried that his son will replace him, and this is what motivates him to attempt to kill his own child. It seems more like a father–son complex to me than a mother–son problem. Why doesn't the father protest the prophecy? Why does Freud choose to ignore the father's conscious and cruel behavior toward his son?

In working as a psychotherapist with couples who have young children, I find that the Oedipal theme of paternal jealousy is common. Many men were the primary focus of their mate's attention prior to the birth of their child. New fathers often report feelings of jealousy because of all the attention the baby is getting and the neglect they feel as a result. New fathers often have a conscious wish to go back to the relationship they had before the baby was born. Helping couples develop into a family and adjust to being parents requires having fathers come to terms with these feelings of jealousy, abandonment and lack of attention from their mates.

I think it is time to re-examine the Oedipal myth in terms of what it is saying about a father's unconscious feelings regarding the early stages of parenthood. The fear of a son or daughter becoming the primary recipient of his mate's attention and affection, and the possibility that the child will replace him as the "king" within the family, are very difficult concepts for a new father.

In Freud's interpretation, fathers can displace their own emotional difficulties onto their children and then punish them for the normal loving relationship that exists between mothers and children. Projecting onto innocent children the feeling of wanting to murder their father for desiring their mother's love appears to me to reflect more on a father's fears and jealousies than anything else.

As fathers today, we need to recognize the mythology that has guided our development. As we create a new definition of fatherhood, we must examine the fears and educate ourselves about aggressive feelings that becoming parents stirs within us. We must come to terms with our own emotional projections and breathe new meaning into a mythology that honors our children and mates. It may not be an easy task to reflect on our own emotional vulnerabilities, but it is one we can help each other with as we grow and develop in our relationships and lives.

FOR FURTHER SELF-REFLECTION AND DISCUSSION

1. Are you jealous of the relationship between your partner and your baby? If so, how does the jealousy manifest itself?

2. How do you handle the frustration when your child's needs must come before your needs?

3. When you were growing up, how did your mother and father reconcile their needs as individuals and as a couple with your needs as a child?

9

THE RITES OF SPRING: HARDBALL, SOFTBALL, AND GENDER

For the last six years I have been involved in coaching boys' Little League and girls' softball. Everything starts in January, when I fill out the application and make sure it gets mailed on time. Then I look at the team schedule for the season and figure out how I will adjust my schedule for the ten to twelve weeks of the season. Being a psychotherapist, I work two evenings a week. When the baseball season starts, I have to modify my evening schedule in order to be able to go to practice and then return to work for a couple of late-evening sessions. Perhaps if I were richer or more financially successful, I would not have to work those evenings. Unfortunately, as a result of the difference between the cost of living in the San Francisco Bay area and my wife's and my wages, I can't afford to lose the income from working those evenings. As in the stories I hear from so many fathers, we all learn to stretch ourselves to try and meet both the emotional and financial needs of our families.

Coaching baseball and softball is my most enjoyable "stretch." I am not a particularly avid fan of professional baseball, but the excitement of watching my children and their friends reminds me of all that is good and noble and engrossing about our national pastime. Both boys and girls bring to the game an energy and intensity that is very captivating and inspiring, and that their professional counterparts seem to lack. The lessons of life — working as a team, trying your best, learning how to lose, improving from your mistakes, enjoying personal success and sharing the pride of winning with friends — are all values that children's sports can bring us in contact with. The openness and naivete that each child brings to the game challenges me as a coach to respond with equal sensitivity to his or her honest emotions.

Observing the difference between girls' softball and boys' hardball allows me to see how gender differences are tied to the social conditioning that we are subject to.

Observing the difference between girls' softball and boys' hardball allows me to see how gender differences are tied to the social conditioning that we are subject to. Also, it is sad to see how boys are pushed to compete and win in order to prove their competence. I was not surprised to see that over 90% of the boys don't continue in organized sports after finishing Little League. I can remember when I played Little League thirty-five years ago. My coach interrogated me after I struck out because, he said, I did not show enough anger. I said I had tried my best, to which he responded that if I didn't get more upset after I struck out, he would take me out of the starting lineup. The next time I struck out I threw the bat against the bat rack, and the coach consoled me for my good try! I had obviously impressed him with my phony display of anger. It seemed as though this incident had convinced him that I had an intensity for the game.

As I began my Little League coaching career in AAA ball, the beginners' level, I went to view an upper-division game to see how it was coached. I was astonished to hear how the coach talked to the boys. Now, being a psychotherapist has its drawbacks, and perhaps having a natural interest in children's development makes me a bit more sensitive to how people communicate. But the criticism that was being leveled at the boys seemed extreme. When we began our season, I noticed distinct differences among coaching styles. Some of the men were without a doubt interested in supporting the boys at whatever level they could play, but others thought that winning was what it was all about. I was sure that I would be in the former group.

The only problem is that the final score never really tells you who won the game.

After our team lost its first four games, however, I found myself getting frustrated and wanting for my team to be "winners." It became easier to be disappointed in the boys when they missed a grounder, and harder and harder not to be discouraged after a poorly played inning. I found myself getting annoyed if the boys didn't play their hardest in each inning. I started to wonder what had happened to my own sensitivity and compassion. Where had I lost the conviction that it was just a game, and how had it become a contest? It was easy to get caught up in what I have always been trained to do, to be a "winner." The only problem is that the final score never really tells you who won the game. It took me years to learn this about life. I knew that I would like to be able to teach this to the children. Slowly, the art of coaching evolves, usually with the teamwork of the coaching staff. In Little League, it took working together and positive reinforcements from each coach on our team to preserve the fun in the game.

I was surprised to see how critical the boys were of each other. A strike or a missed grounder was often met with laughter or a put-down. It took some time for the boys to learn to comfort each other. This was sad for me to see. When the boys were assured that they could comfort a friend who cried when he struck out, the feeling of being a team began to develop. Our society asks boys to be very independent and very competitive early in their lives. I think this makes it harder for them to be supportive of each other. To express their benevolent feelings for each other means showing tenderness and emotion. Boys are told that to be independent, they must give up this tender side of their characters. Being good means achieving "mastery" for boys — and this relates to being in control of their emotions. I think I was a good coach for the Little League because I took a positive stand and said that it was OK to cry and to be upset and to have your friends reassure you. Mind you, not all the coaches supported my position that winning wasn't what it was all about. But it certainly helped with my group's team spirit.

Coaching has challenged me to look at my own values about competition and winning.

In my experience, girls' softball is a completely different story! Being involved with my daughter's softball teams during the last few years has been a real eye-opener, showing me how positive sports can be. The league is organized around the idea that the game is fun. The coaches work cooperatively, and men and women coach together. The spirit of the girls as a team is present from the first day. The girls I have coached are in the second, third and fourth grades. I think two experiences I have had in coaching these girls sum up the differences between coaching the girls and coaching the boys.

First, I discovered that the girls do not want to get their friends "out" on the other teams. Last year, we had to spend the better part of one practice — an hour and a half — talking about how it feels to "make an out" on a friend. I also found that if a girl gets hurt on the field, all the other girls run to her and try to help. We had to ask that just the two or three girls closest to her help out, to keep some order during the game. The sentiment of concern for teammates runs high. The social spirit of the game is intense and the competitiveness I have seen seems to stem more from good fun and "sport" than the values of winning or losing. The sense of mastery through winning does not appear to be a strong motivation in girl's softball.

I know that I have oversimplified much of what goes on in Little League and girls' softball. The point could be made that boys might gain from being less competitive and more team-oriented, and that girls could use a little more stimulation in the competitive realm. Of course, any of you who have coached know that coaching a team involves not only working with the children but working with the parents as well. The parents usually present the greater challenges. Coaching has challenged me to look at my own values about competition and winning. Sharing the experience with my kids has helped us all learn and struggle with what it means to be a team — which, come to think of it, is not so different from what it means to be a family!

FOR FURTHER SELF-REFLECTION AND DISCUSSION

1. How does competition affect boys' relationship to each other?

2. How do we create equal opportunity for our daughters to be physical, assertive and competitive?

3. What are your feelings about the importance of being part of a team? Do you feel that exercise and staying in shape are important?

10

Raising Sons

Our son Morgan is 19 now. Since his birth I have actively participated in his care. This has not always been easy. I think my first lesson was that men as fathers are expected to help their wives but not be too interested in actually caring for their children. Fathers should be helpful around the house but not wander too far into "women's territory."

When Morgan was a baby, I worked only part time so that I could share equally in his care. We made daily journeys to the park. We played in the sand with his trucks and talked with the moms who were there. Because I was the only man at the park with my kid, the consensus or assumption was that I was taking care of my child because I was unemployed.

I remember talking with a grandmother who was at the park. I told her that my wife and I both worked part time, that we didn't need to hire childcare and that I felt fortunate to be able to spend this time with my son, especially while he was a baby. She listened attentively. As I left the park she told me how much she had enjoyed talking with me — and said she hoped I would be able to get some work soon!

I lost count of the number of times women said how nice it was to see a man "mothering." I usually responded that they were actually observing fathering. I was not attempting to be a role model or make a political statement about men as fathers. I was taking action on what was important and meaningful to me.

So this was my first lesson. Procreation was part of being a man. Feeling one's potency through conception, this was definitely masculine. Yet wanting to care for a baby — no, this was not what being a man was about. At least that was the message I was getting. But that was just the beginning.

These early years with my son were wonderful and exciting — and like living with a Zen master. Morgan, like all young children, lived totally in the present. With him I learned about plants, bugs, flowers, cracks in the cement, and all the little details of life and our environment that usually passed me by.

It was when Morgan entered school that I got my real insight into what it means to grow up male in America. Just go to any elementary school and it is easy to ascertain how different boys and girls are. It also became evident that active and energetic boys are sometimes troubling for teachers. They can't sit still. Their curiosity is insatiable, and most teachers (who are usually women) may not be tolerant of their exuberance.

Morgan had studied Martin Luther King and the Civil Rights Movement in the second grade. On our way home from school one day, Morgan told me that in his class the boys were being treated like the blacks in the South whom Martin Luther King was trying to help. I asked him what he meant. He said that if the girls talked out of turn or didn't listen, the teacher would ask them to please be quiet. If the boys did the same thing, she would yell at them and be very angry about how bad they were.

Shaming starts early. To be a man in America means to grow up with a large dose of shame — shame about your energy and desire and shame about your body. Morgan's experiences began to remind me of what I had heard so often in school as a child: "You're too excited and you can't sit still. What's wrong with you that you can't sit still?" What was wrong with me because I got too excited? Why was it bad to feel this way? What a terrible body I must have, that I couldn't sit without moving. If the words themselves weren't shaming, the tone was.

To be a man in America means to grow up with a large dose of shame

Morgan has learned many wonderful things in school, and he has developed and worked out many important relationships. He has had great, mediocre, and bad teachers. My wife and I have tried to guide him to situations that were socially and academically life-enhancing. I would be in denial not to say that boys are treated very differently in school than girls are (at least at the elementary level). And so much of our creativity and feeling is shamed out of us. The exuberance of a third- or fourth-grade boy is a dangerous experience.

The next insight into what it means to be a man has to do with competition. I am amazed and appalled by the level of competitiveness I see among young boys. It begins with athletics and then permeates all other aspects of their lives. What I see is that by the fourth grade a pecking order — a hierarchy — is already established. That hierarchy seems to grant each child a limited potential range of feelings and expression. It is the beginning of our life-long experience with isolation from our peers. In my son's case, I see the absence of adult males in any other area than athletics. There are so few men in the schools to model other ways of being and feeling.

The competitiveness goes far beyond athletics. Who has the best new toy? Whether it concerns a new book or a new Nintendo game, there is a real lack of appreciation for the other boy's experience. It becomes threatening to these eight- and nine-year-olds if a friend has something of value.

How well that translates to my experience as an adult male and the difficulty I see in myself, sometimes, in being able to support and appreciate the achievements of other men! I understand this intellectually, but on the level of feeling it goes deep. Watching my son's experience with his friends, it is obvious how I acquired these feelings.

At Morgan's ninth birthday party he had ten of his friends sleep over. In the morning, the "gang," as we called ourselves, walked to the bakery. On the way home, one of the boys tripped on the sidewalk and fell. He was crying. Immediately everyone laughed and made fun of him. They had learned it is shameful to cry and were shaming their friend with laughter. I held the hurt boy. I called all the other boys around me. I told them that the men I know would help out a friend if he was hurt. I said "real" men would show their strength by caring about what happened to a friend.

I was not prepared for their response. They began to ask their crying friend where his hurt was. They crowded around and put their arms around him. As we continued to walk home, each boy talked with him individually about his tripping on the sidewalk. The whole interaction shifted, and I don't think it was due to the "eloquence" of what I had said.

It became apparent that these boys had absorbed what I said as if it were water and they had been walking through a desert. They thirsted for some validation from an adult male who would say that it is all right to have concerned feelings for a hurt friend. It's OK to cry. I am sure they all knew the loneliness of being teased when they got hurt. I just told them that men care about their friends and show concern about what happens to them. A simple message.

Where are the men — fathers, brothers, uncles, cousins, neighbors, mentors, political leaders and teachers — to carry this simple message to our children?

The shaming, the competitiveness we experience as children, cut us off from appreciating ourselves and others. My son has, through his journey, reminded me of how painful a process it is for boys to grow up in America. I hope that by participating in his life I have helped him to develop some skillful means for finding antidotes to shaming and competitiveness. By being present in his life, and with the help of my male friends, I hope he will see a wide range and depth of feeling experienced and expressed by different men.

The shaming, the competitiveness we experience as children, cut us off from appreciating ourselves and others.

Perhaps growing up male in America is basically an abusive experience. We as men can help each other recover from our shame and competitive/isolating lives. (Much has been said about this in the recent men's movement.) Let us begin our own healing by respecting and nurturing the sons, daughters and children that we know.

FOR FURTHER SELF-REFLECTION AND DISCUSSION

1. Were you made to feel shame as a boy for your male energy?

2. Do you remember any similar situations from your boyhood involving crying — yourself or another?

3. Can men be strong, tender and masculine at the same?

11

FINDING TIME FOR FATHERHOOD

It has been most difficult to find the time to write this essay! When our two children were little, it was obvious why it was impossible to get much private time. Day-to-day tasks were like digging a hole in the sand on the beach: no matter what size the hole, the water would fill it up. The demands of being both physically and emotionally present for infants and young children is pretty much full-time work for both parents.

Now that our children are older (16 and 19), I am surprised that parenting responsibilities are still a major focus of our everyday lives. With each year of fatherhood, I have had to ask myself, "What kind of father do my children need this year?" I have been lucky in that my personal interests and professional career have been interwoven. When coaching and counseling parents with young children I have focused on how to balance parenting with working at jobs and careers. This is an issue I constantly struggle with myself — and am not always satisfied with the results.

As parents, time is our most valuable resource, our most precious commodity. Think about it. We work all our lives so we can retire — so we can do what we want with our time — and the way we define or spend our time defines who we are and what we value.

Our society sets values on the way we use time that have always offended me. In the United States, you can receive a tax credit if you work and place your children in childcare. If you stay at home with your children, however, or work part-time, there is no tax credit. What we say in the U.S. is that we value only the time you spend working. It sends a strong message that parenting is not a priority.

As parents, time is our most valuable resource, our most precious commodity.

We do not need to be locked in a battle between time spent working and time spent parenting. Both work time and family time sustain us in very important ways, and we gain unique satisfactions from both. There are practical matters to consider as well: we need money to live, yet our children are little for such a short time. How will we prioritize our choices?

How we choose to prioritize our time as fathers is very difficult. There is still an unspoken assumption in our society linking our identity as men with our work. Although this is changing, careers still provide men with more esteem, status and financial reward than the time they spend parenting. Also, it is still accepted that the money a man makes is the way he supports his family.

Most of the expectant and new fathers I work with are terribly conflicted by wanting to spend time with their young children while having to cope with the financial pressures. When both parents work, dads as well as moms want more time with their young children. I think we have a much larger social problem then we are aware of in terms of the emotional cost for both parents and young children when it comes to the use of time in the early years of parenthood.

Being a father is now more central to our identity as men, but this is causing problems and repercussions in the work world. Many employers stigmatize new dads, assuming they are less committed to their work than men who don't have children. An attitude that men are less capable if they need to take time off for school activities or medical visits can discriminate against the working dad.

What I think is happening is not that men value work less, but that fatherhood is becoming equally important. While work was once the only source of meaning for a man, fatherhood and parenting have become as important to his self-esteem as his work.

Being a father is now more central to our identity as men, but this is causing problems and repercussions in the work world.

This development parallels the progress that women have made during the last twenty-five years, with an interesting twist. While women have expanded their identity beyond the role of motherhood — exploring the possibilities of new roles in modern society — men are exploring new possibilities and larger roles within the family. They seek the potential to be more emotionally and physically available to their children. As women have moved increasingly into the world of work, men desire to play a bigger role in the world at home.

As dads we need to examine our desires and expectations. If we are socialized to believe self-worth is dominated by our relationship to careers, then we have a conflict when we become fathers and find ourselves wanting to be part of our children's lives. More and more men are choosing to be fathers, and making the necessary financial sacrifices to be involved in family life will require a change in the "culture of work." We need to find ways to be nurturing and involved fathers while making important contributions in the workplace.

From my perspective as a family therapist, it is easy to understand that the changes couples and babies go through in the first year of life depend on having the necessary time to form the attachments that normally occur. Yet we do little as a society to protect this time for parents or children. Pressures mount quickly for parents to get back to work. I am not saying that every couple should stay home with their new baby. What I am saying is that, especially in the early years, there is a need for flexibility in regards to time so that fathers, mothers and babies can have enough time to get to know each other. It takes time to come to a personal understanding of what parenthood and family life mean for each of us as individuals.

In some ways the public problem we have — that we don't provide enough support for families — must be resolved in a private way. Each of us, as a parent and as part of a couple, needs to find the way to create the work–family balance that can sustain our families emotionally as well as financially. We as fathers need to support each other in parenthood. We dads must give each other the encouragement to take risks both emotionally and financially in order to be more integrated in our families.

In choosing our priorities we make sacrifices, but the sacrifice is easy if we recognize the gain. Fathers are being sold a bill of goods whenever we are told that our work will give us all the fulfillment we need in life. We are now discovering that we need to feel connected with our children and families to be truly content. No father on his deathbed has every said, "I wish I had spent more time at work."

We are coming to understand as fathers that our relationships with the important people in our lives — especially our children — are of paramount importance to feeling good about ourselves and feeling that our lives have meaning.

When I asked my children what they think makes a good parent, they gave me the following responses:

Our 16-year-old daughter said that taking your kids to school and picking them up (on time), as well as having time to play with them and help them with their homework, was important. She also commented that young children should spend more time with the parents than with a baby sitter.

Our 19-year-old son summed it up by saying that it just takes time to spend with your kids. He said people should not be prejudiced against teenage fathers — that if they have the time to spend with their kids, they can be good fathers too. It all comes down to time.

I know from the dads and new parents I work with that balancing our many needs and desires while finding the time can often be overwhelming. The same is true for my wife and me. I encourage you not to give up the struggle, however. Finding time for your children is extremely important, because it will not only benefit their development but, particularly for us fathers, make all the difference in how we feel about what is of real value and meaning in life.

Like the seasons of the year, our lives as parents — as fathers — go through transitions. Look at the time you spend with your children in relationship to the season of their lives. Getting your son or daughter off to a good start often takes more time and is very intense. I can't remember how many times I've heard, "They are only little for such a short time." I can't remember any days (or nights) that were longer than when our son and daughter were between birth and two years old. Today I can already feel they have one foot out of our house and the other into lives of their own, and I could not be prouder of each of them. Our life has been wonderful as well as difficult, but more than a few times I have wished we could go back in time and my children could be our babies once again.

Eight Important Considerations for Fathers:

1 From birth onward your physical presence is important to your child. Understand how "being there" for your children often means saying little but standing in the audience, sitting in the bleachers or driving the carpool.

2 Listen, listen, listen and listen to everything your children want to tell you. As they get older take seriously their positions, ideas and opinions.

3 Whether married or divorced, work with your partner for your child's well-being. When differences arise, as they will, try and work things out thinking about the example you are setting for your children.

4 At whatever age, stage or phase your children are at, play with them. Learn to be part of their world of play based on their interest. Whether playing dolls, collecting baseball cards, reading a novel or a comic book, watching TV, going on walks, riding bikes, building sand castles — allow yourself to be led by your child in the joy of playing together.

5 As your children grow, learn about their friends and their families. Try to build bridges with your children's friends' families.

6 Try (knowing you will make mistakes — and be kind to yourself) to live a life that shows your child that hope and opportunity and possibilities exist for them in their lives. Your life is an example of this optimism about life.

7 When in the best interest of your child, say no. Trust that although your children may not always feel positively toward you, know you are doing what is in their best interest. This is the most difficult aspect of fatherhood.

8 Try to keep a sense of humor. There are many opportunities to become depressed as the pressures of life increase as your child grow up. Be conscious of your attitude. Is life a burden or a challenge for you? Consider how this affects your children.

FOR FURTHER SELF-REFLECTION AND DISCUSSION

1. How did your father balance work and family life?

2. How have your routines changed once you had a child? (Or, if you are expecting a baby, how will your routines change?)

3. Can you have different priorities at different times in life?

---12---

DADS AND EDUCATION

As September approaches and summer draws to an end, parents begin to prepare their children (and themselves) for school. I can still remember my son's first day at kindergarten, fifteen years ago. Taking him to school, my wife and I were nervous as we reassured him that school would be fun. We often referred to Sesame Street and how Big Bird was afraid on the first day of school, too. We were proud as well as anxious about this important beginning and transition. All the parents escorted their children to the class, which would be in session from eight to twelve o'clock. The room was brightly decorated with craft projects, a large alphabet around the tops of all four walls, art easels and boxes of puppets and dress-up clothes. It really felt upbeat and fun! Then the parents went for coffee and tea with the principal in an assigned room. The principal reassured us that in his fifteen years of being principal of this school, every single parent had made it through the first day just fine!

Participating in school activities with my children, escorting field trips, being a room parent, being a helper in the class and assisting with school fairs and fund-raising have all been rich experiences for me as a father. They have helped me to feel as though I were a part of a community and have introduced me to many new friends I would not have otherwise met.

Aside from my eighth-grade, high-school and college graduations, I never saw my father or any other father that I can remember at school activities. I think my involvement with my own children has helped me to heal my own loneliness and longing for my father to show an interest in my activities. I also believe that my children have benefited enormously from my participation. School and all the activities associated with it take up an enormous amount of every child's life. The interest you show in what is a major part of their lives — a part that can also cause them worry and fear — comforts them by showing them that you care.

My involvement with my own children has helped me to heal my own loneliness and longing for my father to show an interest in my activities.

Participating in my children's schooling has let them know that I value their education, that school is important and that I make it a priority in my life. It has been reassuring for them to have a father who is familiar with the children in their class, and I believe that it has allowed them to feel more comfortable in school. I feel that my involvement in the early years of my children's education helped them feel more confident in school. In fact, research in the field of child development shows that there is a positive correlation between fathers' involvement in their children's education and their children's academic and social development.

Oftentimes, in working with fathers in my psychotherapy practice, I find that dads have their hearts in the right place, but they may impress their children as too rigid in their desire to help. The dad's need to see his child be successful sometimes overshadows the needs of his child.

I consulted with our (then) fourteen-year-old son on this subject, and he gave me some interesting insights. Morgan thought that being supportive did not always mean helping out with the specifics of homework. He believed that listening to what he was doing and how he was doing it, without too much input, was most valuable. Mistakes would be there, but the overall experience of my interest and excitement about his work was better than helping with a lot of corrections. Great advice from a fourteen-year-old, certainly for dads of adolescents!

I have been very fortunate to have had the experience of being able to play an active role in my children's education. Many other fathers I know would like to be more involved but are prevented from doing so. For various reasons, fathers cannot always do all the things they would like to do for their children. Many questions arise: Where can sacrifices be made, what trade-offs can be made, and how much money can be given up for the time that would be gained? If parents work less and participate more

> *It is simple to say that fathers should be more involved in their children's education, but many dads have difficulty arranging this.*

in their children's early years, how does that affect their ability to save for their children's college years or provide for their own needs later in life?

I have found that it is simple to say that fathers should be more involved in their children's education, but many dads have difficulty arranging this. I am sure that all of the men who attend my programs for fathers would like to be able to spend more time with their children, especially in terms of involvement with their children's education. It appears to me that parents' economic class levels determine how much or how little they can be involved directly with their children. Self-employed professionals seem to have more flexibility than blue-collar workers or corporate employees, for example, while parents in management or ownership positions seem to be able to create more flexible hours. Society in general tends to discount fathers' interest in their children and to pay little attention to the difficulties they may have in balancing their work lives and their home lives.

No matter how busy their schedules are, parents need to rearrange them to allow some time each day to be with their children and to be their children's guides and mentors. Supporting children in their schoolwork and formal education is certainly an important area, but there are also many opportunities in day-to-day life for parents to share their knowledge and to educate their children. Reading to your child at night, looking at the newspaper together and going to movies and plays are all ways of bringing about stimulating discussions between you and your child. Parents have many unique experiences and interests, all of which can enrich their children's lives.

If possible, it's great to be involved at your child's school. Young kids, especially, love to see their dads at school. One year I was a room parent for Julia's third-grade class and loved being an integral part of her day-to-day school life. Several other dads I know came regularly to help out in class. Field trips, school festivals and back-to-school nights are also opportunities to be part of your child's education in an important community, rather than academic, way.

Finally, express your interest in education by continuing to educate yourself. Lectures, classes, reading books and talking about your own new learning are powerful incentives for your children. Look for small opportunities to share educational experience together. (Museums, art galleries, and community centers are often good resources.)

FOR FURTHER SELF-REFLECTION AND DISCUSSION

1. When you were growing up, what was your parents' attitude toward education?

2. How do you help prepare your child for school emotionally?

3. How can you participate in your child's education?

$$\boxed{13}$$

DADS AND DIVORCE

Divorce and parenthood are common occurrences in today's world. The current research on separation and divorce and its effects on children are not definitive. We do know that divisiveness and hostility between parents create emotional conflicts for children. And this is true whether the parents are married or divorced. But every family and every parent–child relationship is unique and has too many variable human factors to project the outcome of the child's self-esteem, personality, or success in life simply because their parents were divorced.

At the millenium, post-divorce fathering still needs to be better understood. There is still an unconscious prejudice about the father's interest and involvement with his children after divorce. It has been my experience from my clinical work that many fathers actually improve the quality, consistency, and interest in their children when faced with the realities of divorce. Divorce defines their time and involvement with their children in a way that the nuclear family may marginalize by having the mother be the presumed "default," who sees to it that their needs are met. It is often after divorce that dads know in detail about student–parent conferences, dates, and times of activities — and do take charge of those things for their children that they may have conveniently left for their wives to do when married.

The focus of this book has been how to recognize the important emotional challenges you face as a father. If you have recognized some of these challenges in earlier chapters, you probably have been conscious about your parenthood and its importance to both you and your children. Just keep up the good work! Trust that you have been an important part of your child's life and nothing can change that. But be aware of these dangers during the divorce process.

Voluntary custody agreements are often far better than court-ordered arrangements. It also shows your child that even with the difficulties that exist between you and your partner that when it comes to their best interest you can work together. Second, avoid the "Disneyland Dad" syndrome. This is where we as fathers feel guilty, or that we need to win our child's favor, so we overindulge them. If you have had a positive relationship with your child, trust in your connection and love and know that they will want to be with you. Of course, the age of your child at the time of divorce will be important. The developmental needs of a six-year-old will be very different from those of a sixteen-year-old.

Divorce appears to be the greatest challenge fathers face. Just the thought of your child being in "custody" of one parent or the other has a bad feeling to it. (Isn't "custody" what happens to suspected criminals?) And the thought of asking permission from a former spouse to be with your child — not easy. The hurt and anger that may develop in divorce can contaminate your ongoing relationship with your child. Finding the best way to be with them may be hard, and the option of giving up and drifting apart often seems like the way to minimize the frustration and anger of a difficult divorce. If you have built an ongoing relationship with your child, then they know you are their father and an important person in their life. If you have not had as close a relationship as you may have wished, then a regular schedule after divorce may help you become a larger part of your child's life.

The idea that when we get divorced we are now "single" needs to change.

Finding satisfaction as a divorced dad takes work. Both your outer and inner worlds are changing. Refocusing your priorities between your work and parenting schedules; thinking about your life apart from marriage; integrating your friends, other potential mates, former in-laws and grandparents — all these are challenges and relationships you need to reflect on. And we live in a culture that has rewarded men for economic and career success, not for emotional and nurturing behavior. All that needs to change in an obvious way as a divorced dad. Your nursing, emotional side needs to rise to the demands of providing for your child. You will be on your own to comfort and calm your child both physically and emotionally when they are with you.

The idea that when we get divorced we are now "single" needs to change. We are never really single people; we are always part of a family. It may be a family of biological relationships, or one of friends, but we are never just a person without a context. That is always true when you are a father. But divorce often brings up many contradictory feelings as a result of the loss of the daily routines, the familiarities, that give our life connections. But there can also be the relief of knowing that, for whatever reasons your relationship with your spouse could not continue, you can now use this profound life change as an opportunity for new possibilities for you and your child. The future may seem uncertain, but who is to say that this uncertainty is not actually filled with potential.

Five "strategies" for making the most of being a divorced dad:

1 Divorce happens — your fault, her fault, or no one's fault. Life is filled with change. Uncertainty is frightening. Care about yourself, admit the loss and guilt and frustration, sorrow and relief and joy that divorce inspires in all of us. Take pride and gratitude in being a father. DO NOT SHAME YOURSELF because your marriage didn't work out. You will discover that you are still part of a family, just a different one!

2 Remember — divorce is between spouses, not parents and children. Continue to develop your relationship with your child. It may be more difficult, but be creative. Know that you can trust in your ability to let your child know that you love them, are there for them, and, most important, enjoy being with them.

3 You will now be developing a family system independent of your previous family. It will be different. Normalize your life with your child around your new routines.

4 Your child needs you and you need your child. As time goes on there will be many activities and adventures you will participate in with your child. School, sports, their friends, buying clothes, preparing meals — all the myriad of actives that help frame their lives from preschool to college.

5 Listen more closely to your child's feelings as you make the transition from a nuclear family to a new model of family life.

Give your kids the permission to feel whatever they are feeling with your support. And take care of yourself. It will mean so much to your child to know that you can cope with the changes that lie ahead. It will reassure them that things will be manageable for them to know that their parents are stable. And remember the stability I am talking about is not about money and possessions, but about the heart and the emotions.

FOR FURTHER SELF-REFLECTION AND DISCUSSION

1. Have there been any divorces in your family?

2. What about getting divorced is most frightening or upsetting for you?

3. What potential improvements may come for your child/children from divorce?

| 14 |

PATERNITY AND PEACE

Paternity and peace —people oftentimes feel these words are contradictory. Is the patriarchal model of Western society at the root of our international conflicts? Perhaps there is some degree of truth here, especially if we are to identify our images of what it means to be a man with the likes of John Wayne, Rambo, or the image created by the gladiator and so-called professional wrestling television shows.

If you look at the images of men presented by the media, what do you see? Violent heroes, murderers, rapists and assorted criminals make up much of the day-to-day reporting on men in the news as well as the casts of most television shows. Men featured in commercials usually alternate between the young macho-car-driving types and the incompetent males who can't do simple household chores.

I am surprised that more men and fathers don't take offense at these pejorative characterizations. In the mid-60s, women began to respond to the stereotypes society had cast for them. Why haven't men followed suit today?

The issue of violence and world peace takes on new meaning when we become fathers, however. Many dads I have worked with talk about the apprehension they feel for their children in today's world. Thirty years ago parents worried that their kids might play hooky from school. Fifteen years ago parents worried about marijuana. Today's parents worry that their kids might be shot! The increase in school violence exemplified by the Columbine shootings has made many parents unsure about their children's basic daily safety.

Eric Erickson, the noted child psychiatrist, describes men who desire children as developing into the "generative" phase of psychosocial development. This developmental period is characterized by a greater and more profound interest in how the course of external events will affect the lives of others.

The issue of violence and world peace takes on new meaning when we become fathers.

A special sense of compassion and social awareness is born with fatherhood. It seems almost biological in nature; so many new fathers appear to be vulnerable to events they might have ignored before they become dads.

This new caring opens the door for men to examine a deeper and more personal issue. As we encounter the difficulties and frustrations of understanding our new identities as fathers, we may experience feelings of anger and rage. Perhaps we had a father who expressed his anger in ways we think was destructive, yet we find ourselves imitating his behavior despite our good intentions. Maybe we had a physically abusive or alcoholic father, and now we can see how his behavior has influenced us. Our fathers' ability to understand and express anger and rage is the legacy we inherit as we become fathers.

How do we teach peace to our children? How can we help the world choose the path of peace rather than the path of war? As corny as it sounds, peace begins at home. When we as fathers understand our own anger and rage, we can begin to end this self-defeating legacy of violence that is passed on from generation to generation.

Joseph Chilton Pierce commented that it is not how many nuclear bombs we have that scares him, but rather who it is that can decide to push the button. It will be the next generation — our children — who are faced with the difficult decisions between peace and violence. Much of the knowledge they will use to choose between cooperation and conflict will come from their fathers.

FOR FURTHER SELF-REFLECTION AND DISCUSSION

1. Be self-reflective; consider how you express your anger and frustration.

2. Do you think it is appropriate to display anger in front of your children?

3. How do you calm yourself down when you get upset or things don't work as you have planned?

$$\boxed{15}$$

FATHERHOOD AND
THE MEN'S MOVEMENT

One of the lasting changes that came out of the 1960s was the Women's Movement. What women began as a revolution, however, has become an evolution. Both women and men are continuing to move away from traditionally defined gender roles. While these role changes have perhaps been more visible for women, men are moving at their own pace towards new possibilities. The changes in role expectations are opening up a new world for men who want to be fathers. The egalitarianism that is now possible among couples allows men to express their deep desire and ability to nurture and care, which were earlier subject to social disapproval.

Men now feel that they have a choice between spending time at work, and taking time to be with their children while they grow up. Men who are able to take advantage of this possibility began to report a very deep feeling of satisfaction as well as personal growth, which they experience by being with and caring for their babies. As other men view this new role-making behavior, and hear men recount the peak experience of being present at their children's birth, the notion of becoming a father begins to take on new meaning.

In the new potentials of being fathers, men see the possibility to express themselves through nurturing; there appears to be something very attractive about this for many men. Maybe this nurturing quality has been dormant within us for decades. Perhaps watching our children being born triggers some ancient biological process. As men spend more time with their children, new images of what it means to be a "real man" are being created.

What is going on in the men's movement? Do we really need a movement? Since most of the institutions in our society are designed and controlled by men, what is it we really want to change?

War, incest, poverty, racism, and the relationship between men and women are not separate and independent issues but interconnected and part of our social value system.

Any men's movement that does exist owes a great debt to the women's movement and the development of feminist philosophy/psychology in the United States. For more than twenty years women have been championing the causes of equality and equity both in the work world and in family life. They have led the struggle to improve education and childcare.

Any men's movement that does exist owes a great debt to the women's movement and the development of feminist philosophy/psychology.

Today's media-driven men's movement has ignored father-hood. This has been my personal experience as I have partici-pated in groups and workshops over the past twenty-five years. It was one of the reasons for my starting the Fathers' Forum in 1986. In groups with Robert Bly and Michael Mead, and in my own men's groups and activities in Northern California, I found a wonderful community of men. I discovered that the com-petitiveness and isola-tion I was taught to value was keeping me from being part of a community. The losses I carried within and never expressed were slowly eating me up from inside. I began to understand how the un-conscious devaluing of women had cut me off from a more nurturing part of myself. Through

This is the greatest gift of the men's movement — to have the opportunity to safely talk with other men about the inner experiences of day-to-day living.

myth and stories, but mostly in the care of men — some older, some younger — I found a place to tell my stories. I became aware of how little opportunity I had had to talk about life, and the struggles of my own experiences, with other men. This is the greatest gift of the men's movement — to have the oppor-tunity to safely talk with other men about the inner experi-ences of day-to-day living. This is the most healing and politi-cally radical change the men's movement has created.

It was not until I had children myself that I began to realize that the issues of being a father and having a family were not being addressed by my "men's work." Talking about what it means to be a man is important, but if it does not connect us to the greater issues of our lives, then the men's movement is a failure. If the men's movement causes a greater schism between men and women than already exists, then it has failed doubly.

I think the most vital aspect of today's men's movement — and the least publicized and understood — is fatherhood. A fundamental shift is taking place in our society. We are aspiring to transition from a hierarchical to a partnership culture. Here we find that work and home life, making money and raising children, are becoming cooperative ventures by men and women.

What today's fathers are doing all over the country is a grassroots political movement. When men become fathers, an opportunity for a profound and fundamental emotional shift in consciousness arises. The vulnerability of their children can touch their own fears and vulnerabilities, and an emotional awakening can occur. This awakening is not just to the world of feelings. It is a connection to the world of greater political realities that they must now struggle with. It is the experience of "generativity" that carries the father from his own concerns about his identity as a man, to the greater concerns for his family and community.

For years the men's movement has attempted to help men develop from the narcissistic stage of manhood to more dynamic involvement in our society. Today's fathers are fulfilling that aspiration. Our sense of manhood, what kind of person we want to be — beyond gender definition — is what today's dads struggle with. I see it over and over again in my father's groups. Men are reintegrating the nurturing and generative aspects of their emotional lives, and are coming to terms with a new definition of what it means to be a man, a definition which includes how to contribute to a society worthy of bringing children into.

Understanding what it takes to be a parent — the sleepless nights and endless patience, feeling the fears and vulnerabilities of having young children, worrying about education and childcare, figuring out how to provide guidance, setting limits without injuring your child's spirit, living equitably with your partner, being a parent and a husband, crafting a loving marriage and a family with values, morals and ethics — these are the challenges for today's dads. Sharing these struggles with other men/fathers helps create a community of men who are not only raising their consciousness about being men, but about the society we live in.

It is my hope that as the respective men and women's movements continue to develop, we will see that our similarities outweigh our differences. We can live together as allies and raise children who will reflect all the best of what it means to be not just men or women, but truly caring human beings.

FOR FURTHER SELF-REFLECTION AND DISCUSSION

1. What "feminine" qualities do you feel would help you as a man?

2. Are there subtle ways that you devalue women, or do you deal with the men and women in your life equally?

3. Are men and women being socialized differently? How so?

ANOTHER LOOK AT FAMILY VALUES

Less than 100 years ago, 90% of the U.S. population lived on farms. Most were subsistence farms, with the family needing to work together to fulfill the physical necessities of life. The family was also the center for education and learning. Family values were what you learned in the day-to-day working-out of life: understanding the changing seasons and the best time to plant crops or a garden, being able to recognize a good horse, and how to get along with your neighbor. These were the necessities for survival, but they also connected us to a deeper rhythm of life within the environment and our communities. The Bible was a popular tool for teaching reading and for community guidance (i.e., "Do unto others as you would want them to do unto you"), but the majority of Americans were not orthodox in their spiritual practices. The value of teamwork and collaboration in both the family and community was central to survival and to living a civilized life. The rural home was the center of American life and culture; it was the productive center of our society. The farm provided everything needed to live. Survival and success were vitally linked to our relationships with others. It could be said that the value of cooperation within the family and the community, and with the land, was the principal "family value" in America at the turn of the century.

Today, less than 3% of our population lives on farms. Almost all farms today are part of agribusiness. There are few subsistence farms. The home today is not a place of production but the center of consumption. Beginning in the 1920s, industrial development ejected the father from the house into the office or factory. Fifty years later, in the 1970s, just to "maintain" in our society of labor-saving devices and conveniences, mothers joined dads in the work force. The values of a consumer society, based mainly on materialism, slowly became the dominant values for American families.

What I propose is that . . . we revitalize the family-farm value of cooperation.

The satisfaction once experienced in relationships with family members, friends and communities has been replaced by the illusion of satisfaction through owning things. It has become so desirable to have a new car, the fastest computer, the latest CD, the most fashionable clothes, that people believe they will find satisfaction in life by possessing them. Commercial advertising, through the use of sophisticated psychological techniques, attempts to sell us products that will make us believe we are part of the "good life." The price the American family has paid for the good life has led us to be a nation suffering from depression.

We are lonely for each other and for a sense of being part of a greater community.

Many people today long for a sense of community and personal attachment. We live in isolation from friends and family, and the need or desire for cooperation and teamwork as a family value has been replaced by the value of independence and self-sufficiency (especially emotionally). This profound change in the function of the home, from a center of productivity and connection to one of consumerism, has taken its toll on all of us as parents and partners (husbands and wives) but has affected our children most profoundly. Frustrated children, either in school or day care; long hours of watching television; parents exhausted by trying to make ends meet — all of these have led us to our current discussion of family values in America.

Unfortunately, much of the family-values movement offers an oversimplified response to helping our families. There is the mistaken notion that if the fathers are out there making a "good living" and mothers are in the home caring for children, we will regain a sense of balance in our society. Some of the leaders in this new movement try to use the Bible as the ultimate authority on how we need to organize our families. I wish the solution were so easy — that we could just look up what we need to do in a book!

The family has been and is a dynamic living organism. It has changed and adapted in the course of history to many different configurations. It exists today in many different paradigms throughout the world. In America we need to look at our own unique cultural and social conditions and ask ourselves what our families need now.

What I propose is that, on the personal level — on the simplest level — we revitalize the family-farm value of cooperation. Like the couples who ran family farms, we as parents can begin to work together as partners, looking at the demands and chores of life much as the farm families did. We need to ask how we can equitably share the tasks of sustaining a family. From earning our living to doing the laundry, we as parents can figure out how to navigate these tasks together. We can again learn how to reach out to our neighbors and friends, to help each other through the vicissitudes of modern life. We as families can learn to provide an environment in our daily lives that values cooperation and caring. We have to find the time, as families, to enjoy being together and sharing the events that shape our days. We want our children to be able to look to us, their parents, to have the skills and creativity to create a nurturing atmosphere.

The days of the father being at work and the mother staying home with the kids are gone, no longer a realistic model to emulate for parenting. As a family therapist, I often question whether it was ever the best model for raising children. But we have moved into new territory for parenting where, for both the satisfaction of the couple and survival of many families, men and women need to move toward learning how cooperation and teamwork can lead to enjoyment and satisfaction in life.

FOR FURTHER SELF-REFLECTION AND DISCUSSION

1. What is your response to the idea that family values are rooted in the cooperation between husband and wife?

2. What are three of the values that you and your partner convey to your children?

3. What will your child or children learn about family values from watching the relationship between you and your partner?

17

LEARNING FROM
SPECIAL-NEEDS CHILDREN

The United States today is not a society that is supportive of parents or family life. Although politicians would like us to believe otherwise, social connectedness, childcare support and sharing parental information are all very difficult for anyone who has children. The problem is compounded by our jobs, which ask us to compartmentalize our lives so that we are parents at home and employees at work — as if one is not influenced by the other. Mix all the ingredients together in the best of all circumstances, and one must still continually seek creative alternatives to meet the challenges of parenting.

These challenges are increased geometrically for parents of special-needs children. Whether due to accidents, or to genetic or birth problems, these children develop and grow at a different pace than what is rather arbitrarily regarded as normal.

There are many challenges that greet the fathers of special-needs kids. Our socialized emphasis on competition is normally manifested in our desire to have our children meet our needs for success. Fathers of special-needs children, however, have the opportunity to free themselves of preconceptions and expectations and to learn what their children have to offer in other ways. Though the process may be painful and difficult, the evolution of this unconditional love is as great a gift to the father as the child.

At a conference I attended many years ago a woman shared a story about how much she and her husband had wanted a child. Since they had medical problems that did not permit conception, they decided to adopt. They were both successful in their careers and had set up their lives to indulge themselves with their child. The woman spoke of what they had planned — the travelling, the classes in art and music, and the books they would share with their child.

But soon they noticed that he appeared to be developing more slowly than their friends' children, and it was discovered that he had Down Syndrome. Tears came to the woman's eyes as she spoke. She said her son is now 30 years old and a wonderful, loving person. She talked about how difficult it was for her and her husband to give up their hopes for what might have been and to discover the very different and special child who had come into their life for them to love.

Special-needs children teach us all that loving our children is not about who we want them to be, but about who they are.

FOR FURTHER SELF-REFLECTION AND DISCUSSION

1. How is your child different from how you hoped he/she might be?

2. What do you love most about your child?

3. How are you different from what your parents had hoped for you and your life?

18

FOOD FOR THOUGHT

Educating ourselves about parenting is a critical part of our being "good enough" fathers. Understanding the importance of food and the need for independence among small children is basic to helping them develop good eating habits and self-esteem.

Many of the difficulties I see with dads of teenagers and families with adolescents are issues that began in early childhood as struggles around food. As a family therapist, one of the areas I want to discuss when a family comes in for treatment is its food and eating routines.

For young children, how often and how much they eat can vary greatly. Young children's appetites are not organized around the adults' defined eating times. As adults we have learned — as children do over time — to be organized around eating three times a day. Our external and internal rhythms are now structured around these times. Young children are much more internally focused. A three-year-old can want nothing to eat at noon, and be famished by twelve-thirty. A young child focusing on play may find lunchtime (and food) an un-welcome intrusion.

Young children's need for independence is often expressed in an unfocused manner. Eating is one way they may experiment with the confusion. Acting out around food is one way a young child tries to understand and master his need for independence and autonomy. What he puts in his mouth and how much he eats and when he eats are among the few ways he can exercise independent control in his life. Children can eat huge meals one day and not be hungry at all the next. They can love a special food one week and refuse to eat it a week later. Sometimes a child may want to be totally catered to, while at other times the same child may want to be left alone.

> *Young children's appetites are not organized around the adults' defined eating times.*

While all dads would like their children to enjoy eating, each parent brings his or her own hang-ups to this area. Usually there are unresolved issues from our own childhood that we react to in our children. If you remember your own past experiences around eating, you need not continue them with your children. Forcing a child to eat is a certain road to eating problems. In order for a child to enjoy eating, he or she must be in control.

Toddlers will often use food to test limits. They will always want the food you don't have. You can let your child know that "This is what we have for dinner tonight. We will have [whatever the child is asking for] tomorrow night." Parents need to learn to relax around meal times. Children's nutritional needs are fairly simple, and you are probably doing just fine if your child falls within the normal ranges for weight and height and if the available food is generally nutritious.

If you haven't made food a struggle for both you and your children, by the time they are four or five they will find it exciting to try new foods and experiment with new tastes. Establishing independence about eating is one way in which we help our child learn their own limits and foster their ability to make their own choices — an essential ingredient in positive self-esteem. Pickiness, refusal of certain foods, wide variation in tastes from one week to the next, are all part of the normal phases kids go through. Tolerance is what we need to learn — and show — as parents.

If you haven't made food a struggle for both you and your children, by the time they are four or five they will find it exciting to try new foods and experiment with new tastes.

Of course, if your child refuses to eat over a prolonged period or is very thin or overweight, it would be appropriate to seek your doctor's advice.

Respecting our children's need for control, and being aware of our own eating history, we can proceed into the future with our families in a relaxed and positive manner at meal times.

I hope this has given you some food for thought.

FOR FURTHER SELF-REFLECTION AND DISCUSSION

1. What are the "feeling tones" at your meals? Tense or relaxed?

2. How flexible or rigid are you about your child's eating?

3. When you were growing up, what were the rules about food and eating? What was the mood around the dinner table with your parents?

19

CHRISTMAS

The holiday season brings up a variety of feelings for families, from joy to dread. The pressures of our consumer society can make this a tense time of year. Crowded stores and traffic jams all add to the flurry of activity that often pushes us to the limits of our patience. We find ourselves asking the question, Is it really worth it? Could we do without this "holiday madness?" Couldn't we just skip the whole thing?

It is up to us as parents (or us as dads) to rescue Christmas from its commercialism and restore it as one of the special days in our children's lives. We can help create a special time of year to celebrate children, which I believe was the original intent of this holiday.

For most children, Christmas is not a religious holiday. Children don't associate a jolly fat man in a red suit with any religious symbolism. As my daughter once said, it is quite exciting to have a tree in the house. When our children were young, the surprise on their faces when they found their presents under the tree made it clear how special the experience was for them.

Christmas is a celebration of children.

Christmas is a celebration of children. As I researched the history of St. Nick, I was led to his pre-Judeo-Christian past. It appears Santa Claus has his origins in a pre-Christian deity who was the protector of children, a nature spirit similar to the "green man" whose job it was to look out for the welfare of children. Both Hanukkah and Christmas may have been adjusted to coincide with this earlier folk tradition, which was the focus of the winter season.

Children, especially young ones, need to have special days that are just for them. Except for school graduations and religious ceremonies that mark memorable moments in their lives, children have few special days of their own. Only birthdays and Christmas remain as days truly reserved for kids. If these days are diminished in importance, children lose some of life's joy and the good feelings that go with it.

Santa Claus reaches out to children in a unique way. Presents and giving can certainly express love and good will at this time of year. Most children know Santa doesn't bring gifts to parents. Somehow, Santa Claus is just for them. For children who believe in the Santa Claus story, Christmas can be a magical time that brings much personal happiness.

Children who can experience the ancient myth of Santa Claus have their lives immensely enriched. The thought of a good, happy, colorfully dressed person who brings presents just for them creates a sense and magic in their lives. While difficulties and uncertainties in life are many, Christmas and the magic of Santa Claus help reassure children and give them a sense of hope. If our rational thinking forces us to deprive our children of the symbolic meaning that Santa represents, we lose the beneficial effects that can extend over the lifetime of the child.

Children have a need for magical thinking. From about four to ten years old, magical thinking actually helps kids cope with the world. The hardships, difficulties, even terrors that are part of our lives — which we cope with as adults in our own way — can be dealt with by young children through magical beliefs. Magical thinking declines as children grow and their rational consciousness is equipped to deal with the uncertainties and vicissitudes of life.

Together, my wife and I have tried to craft a unique Christmas for our children. We have a great time choosing a tree and decorating it. Our tree is covered with ornaments the kids have made over the years. Our children feel the joy of getting gifts that are given in celebration of them, with no one but Santa to thank.

As our children have gotten older, we have begun to explore the meaning of "peace" at this time of year. This is a time when we can all wish for a world that is more nurturing and peaceful. Our children can begin to express the feelings

If our rational thinking forces us to deprive our children of the symbolic meaning that Santa represents, we lose the beneficial effects that can extend over the lifetime of the child.

of gratitude that reflect their own experience of Christmas and what it means to them.

The winter solstice, the seasonal change, begins to mark a time of turning inward. With less daylight, the cold, the change in the landscape around us, we all feel some of the seasonal transition. Connecting with these changes is part of the experience of Christmas for us, too. My wife and I take pleasure in creating a meaningful time for us to enjoy being a family together.

FOR FURTHER SELF-REFLECTION AND DISCUSSION

1. What do you find most difficult about the holiday season?

2. How did your family celebrate Christmas when you were a child?

3. How would you like to celebrate Christmas, and how can you talk about it with your partner?

20

FATHER'S DAY

When we celebrate Father's Day, what are we celebrating? Is it a personal tribute to our fathers? Is it the commemoration of male parentage? Of all the holidays, Father's Day is one of the least observed and celebrated. Perhaps because men's relationships with their own fathers are often difficult, they feel reluctant to honor a day in their dads' behalf. In my work with fathers, I find that the number of men who want to honor their fathers on this day is equal to the number of men who want to mourn their relationships with their fathers. It seems that Father's Day is a bittersweet national holiday, evoking both the admiration and disdain that men (and women) feel towards their fathers.

As men become fathers, celebrating this day can become very intense emotionally. I feel that men undervalue how profoundly they may be affected by this institutionalized ritual of acknowledging fatherhood. There is much denial in our society and in our personal lives about fatherhood. All men hope for fathers who can support them in both their physical and emotional needs. Young children want to trust the adults who are responsible for them. Parents are often not prepared or are not aware of how to "be there" for their kids.

Being there for your children means giving them your time and attention. Focusing on their needs and feelings, and helping children cope with their disappointments and excitements — this is the core of parenting. And this is true for fathers and mothers both!

What happens to children when their fathers either are not or cannot be there for them? Research indicates that children of absent fathers do less well socially and academically. They may also have more difficulties in interpersonal relationships. It is not just having a male parent in the house that is important. It is the ability of the father to be nurturing, warm and caring for his child. That is what fathering is all about.

We can dedicate ourselves on this Father's Day to transforming the paternal bond between ourselves and our families.

Many men can look back on their lives and find adults who were not their biological dads but who supported them, coached them, and were "mentor fathers." It is natural for children to seek out adults who can take pride in their achievements and convey to them that they are special and unique.

How men interact with their children and their mates, and how they feel about themselves as men, leaves a lasting impression on their children. Children's attitudes reflect the possibilities their parents see for themselves. Children learn the limitations of life and their own potential by watching how their parents deal with daily life — from how they greet the day, to how they cope with disappointment and loss.

As we reflect on Father's Day this year, let us appreciate that, even if we were very wounded by our own fathers, we can be more substantial, more present in our children's lives than we felt our fathers were in ours. We can honor all the fathering influences who have contributed to our lives. We can dedicate ourselves on this Father's Day to transforming the paternal bond between ourselves and our families into a nurturing, cooperative and vital connection. Let us thank our children and let them know how proud we are of them and how lucky we feel to be their fathers on this Father's Day.

FOR FURTHER SELF-REFLECTION AND DISCUSSION

1. What did you do for Father's Day last year?

2. How was Father's Day celebrated when you were a child?

3. How would you like your Father's Day to be acknowledged?

4. Aside from your biological father, who were or are the other "fathers" in your life?

AFTERWORD

I did not write this book. The essays here where inspired by the fifteen years of groups I have been leading for new and expectant fathers. I was just lucky enough to record the moment and develop the ideas. I now encounter in the streets of Berkeley, California some of the "pioneering" fathers who were in my early groups in the late 1980s and struggled along with me making sense and meaning out of becoming a father.

And I am glad to report that we were right — history and time have borne us out! Being a father is truly one of the most worthwhile, creative, and meaningful relationship we can experience in our lives. It was these men who, like the million of loving and nurturing fathers that are actively involved with their children and are largely ignored by the media, are redefining what it means to be a man. The media instead will search for the deadbeat dad or child abuser, and run an hour-long special on a sick and mentally disturbed man who tormented his children, pointing out what this father did. Meanwhile the millions of kind, and caring dads go about their responsibilties as parents inspired by the sheer joy of watching their children grow and develop and be a part of their lives. The development of this new paradigm for fatherhood — the involved and active dad — will be our most significant contribution in this millennium. Yes, the microchip and the incredible technological advance we will see in our lives will be spectacular. And advances in the biological science will improve the health and longevity of our children in so many ways. But the infrastructure of all this will be our families, and the new role fathers are engaged in within the family.

So if you are a father and have just finished this book, you know that the meaning of our lives as men is deeply rooted in our experiences with our children and our ability to struggle with all the difficulties of loving and nurturing them.

Remember we are all part of the great community of fatherhood. Each of us as men has unique insight into how caring for our children has humanized us as men — and is changing the world!

About the Author

Bruce Linton, Ph.D., founded the Fathers' Forum, which offers workshops, classes and groups for expectant and new fathers. Bruce is a licensed marriage, family and child counselor and received his doctorate for research on men's development as fathers. He was a contributing editor to *Full-Time Dads* magazine and a former columnist for *Children's News* in San Francisco. Bruce has a private counseling and psychotherapy practice in Berkeley, California, where he lives with his wife and two children. Bruce is a popular speaker at conferences, hospitals, corporations, and community organizations.